THE RELUCTANT READER

WENDY M. WILLIAMS, Ph.D., is a research scientist at Yale University and a leading authority on childhood reading and learning patterns. In this book she gives you the tools to analyze your child's life—and the strategies to make reading a big part of it. Use this book to:

- See your child for who he or she is—and find out what part reading can play in her life
- Make reading fun—and important—to your child
- Find the right kind of reading material for your child
- Set reading goals
- Make reading a family affair
- Eliminate pressures that keep kids from reading.

THE RELUCTANT READER

HOW TO GET AND KEEP KIDS READING

WENDY M. WILLIAMS, PH.D.
RESEARCH SCIENTIST, DEPARTMENT OF
PSYCHOLOGY, YALE UNIVERSITY

WARNER BOOKS

A Time Warner Company

WARNER BOOKS EDITION

Cover design by Lisa McGarry

Warner Books, Inc.
1271 Avenue of the Americas
New York, NY 10020

Visit our web site at
http://pathfinder.com/twep

W A Time Warner Company

Printed in the United States of America

First Printing: August, 1996

10 9 8 7 6 5 4 3 2 1

For children and parents who love to read.

Acknowledgement

Many thanks to friends and colleagues who contributed ideas, support, and encouragement: at Yale, Melanie Gordon Brigockas and Michel Ferrari; in Litchfield, Margy Eveleth, Ken Miner, and Kuma, who kept me company during long hours of writing. I also thank my agent, Jeff Herman, and Joann Davis of Warner Books for giving me this opportunity.

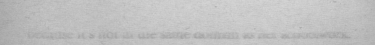

THE
RELUCTANT
READER

PREFACE

Camerado, this is no book.
Who touches this, touches a man.
—WALT WHITMAN

A man's library is a sort of harem.
—RALPH WALDO EMERSON

I read part of it all the way through.
—SAM GOLDWYN

Michelle felt her jaw tighten. She had just returned home from the office to find her daughter
Megan transfixed by the TV again—for the fourth time
this week. Why didn't she ever pick up a book? Michelle
wondered. She thought that Megan would be content
to waste her life in front of that screen. When she was
five, she loved to ask questions about everything; she
seemed so interested in learning. Now, she sat there for
hours like a piece of furniture.

Later that night, Michelle's husband, Mark, asked
why she was so down. "I'm worried about Megan," she
said. "She does well in school, but they don't give much
reading for homework—nothing to really challenge
her. If she had her way she'd spend all her time watch-

1

ing sitcoms and playing computer games. When I was her age I'd spend hours in my room lost in a book. My mother would have to call me three times to come downstairs for dinner. But I've never *once* seen Megan choose to read for the fun of it. She reads stuff for school, but always with the TV on in the background— it's like she's dying to get the book over with. She's never learned to enjoy reading the way we do. I'm afraid it will hurt her down the road."

"I think you're overreacting," Mark said. "She's a bright kid. She'll grow into reading naturally if we give her the time. Besides, kids today just don't read the way their parents did."

Michelle is wise to worry: Kids who read have the edge in school and in life. Countless studies have confirmed the link between children's reading and IQ, school achievement, and motivation. Kids who love to read are kids who love to learn. They're better students, and they profit more from instruction and remember more facts. They know how to get answers to questions and locate and use information. They know more words and speak more like adults from an early age. In general, they know a lot about many different subjects, and their knowledge is broader and more valuable than the knowledge kids get from watching TV and playing video games. Kids who love to read also learn to write sooner and better. Their compositions are more interesting to teachers, so they generally get better grades. Like becoming a good learner, becoming a good writer starts with being a good reader. Reading really does open doors in life.

Michelle's husband is typical of many parents who believe their kids will gravitate naturally toward reading as they grow up. They're wrong. Reading is a habit, and the earlier in life it is acquired, the better. Kids don't magically begin picking up books one day if their home and school experiences don't reinforce the pleasures of reading. Parents have to create the opportunities for reading and support their children in acquiring this essential habit. Like any habit, reading takes practice, but once a kid is hooked she'll stick with it and continue to enjoy its rewards.

This will never be a civilized country until we expend more money for books than we do for chewing gum.
—ELBERT HUBBARD

The reading of all good books is like conversation with the finest men of past centuries.
—RENE DESCARTES

Reading is thinking with someone else's head instead of one's own.
—ARTHUR SCHOPENHAUER

THE RELUCTANT READER

Why do some kids not like to read? Many children who do well in school are never found curled up lost in a book. If you are the parent of a reluctant reader, you can probably remember the worlds that books revealed to you when you were a child. Maybe you remember loving detective stories or romance novels or even comic books—what matters is that they were *books*, and you couldn't wait to devour them. But now your child shies away from books, and you're worried because you know what reading meant to your childhood.

Research shows that your concern is justified—first, because reading is associated with success in most areas of adult life in our society, and second, because reading is a habit children can *learn*. Just because your child is a reluctant reader doesn't mean you should give up: There are proven winning strategies that help. There are also losing strategies that *don't* help, and, paradoxically, these are often the ones parents choose. Why? Because parents create their children's environment, and as a result they are often part of the reading problem. Knowing which strategies will work for your child and using these strategies effectively depends on your knowing *your* role in your child's reading problem. You must understand the dynamic between you and your child and see how this dynamic affects your child's reading behavior. Once you do, this knowledge will help you to change the dynamic and create an environment that enables and encourages reading.

What, specifically, can parents do? And—often more important—what are parents doing wrong? My own and others' work has revealed simple strategies that get kids excited about reading. Through my research at Yale University as Director of the Yale-Harvard Practical and Creative Intelligence for School Project, I've listened to parents, teachers, and children talk about why kids do and don't choose to read. I've heard the problems children face from their own perspective—and I've heard how their parents and teachers see the same situations. I've learned what works to get kids excited about books, and what guarantees that a kid won't pick up a book for at least a month.

The Reluctant Reader shares these and other insights with you, giving you simple, workable strategies to apply today to get your kids excited about reading. The book shows you how to encourage kids to choose to read even when they don't have to. And, just as important, it describes common parental strategies that bomb with kids. *The Reluctant Reader* contains anecdotes and vignettes gathered over years of conversations with parents, teachers, and children. I've written this book with parents in mind: It speaks to you in a voice you can relate to and understand. And when you need an idea to use immediately to get or to keep your child reading, you can turn to the appendix, 75 Quick Ways to Get and Keep Kids Reading.

Here you will gain the knowledge to create a positive reading environment for your child. Here you'll learn about different types of children with different types of reading problems, and what works to help each type of child in each situation. The six children profiled in *The Reluctant Reader* are based on real children I have known. I chose this representative sample to illustrate the many reasons why kids don't like to read. I describe the parents and their misguided though well-intentioned efforts to help their children, and I talk about strategies proven through research to get kids reading and *enjoying* it.

The children described in this book range in age from nine to sixteen. Chapter 1, Ashley's Story, is about a thirteen-year-old seventh grader whose older, successful, career-oriented parents are out of touch with her life. Ashley is a victim of benign neglect, and reading is the primary casualty.

Chapter 2, Ben's Story, is about a sixteen-year-old, eleventh grade computer jock who prefers the high-tech to the high-touch world. His mother has cast him in the role of male family leader, and her unrealistic and inappropriate expectations only make his reading problem worse.

Chapter 3 looks at nine-year-old Laura, a third grader with a fuller schedule than most adult professionals. Laura's life is so overscheduled and overcommitted, it's a wonder she doesn't have an ulcer in addition to a reading problem.

In chapter 4, twelve-year-old Jeremy illustrates the pernicious effects of the bane of so many parents: the dreaded video game! Jeremy has trouble with reading because he spends his spare time playing video games, and because his father doesn't provide the support and direction he needs at home to improve his reading.

Chapter 5, Kim's Story, is about a fourteen-year-old ninth grader who reads just fine—but who would rather paint, act, and write poetry than prepare for the professional career her mother has chosen for her. Kim is reluctant to read the stuff *her parents* want her to read.

Finally, chapter 6 is about ten-year-old Chase, who is paralyzed by fear of failing and not measuring up to his father's extreme expectations. Chase feels dumb even though he isn't, and his reading problem is a direct reflection of his low self-esteem.

These six children, taken together, cover the spectrum of kids with the key, core problems of reluctant readers everywhere. You will probably meet a child or parent in these pages who reminds you of someone in your family. I've found that children's reading problems tend to come in a few basic flavors; that is, we tend to see the same patterns of child-school-family interactions over and over. So, even though I have written about only six children, these girls and boys represent the situations and types of problems that affect most children who don't enjoy reading. You'll likely find yourself and your child in here somewhere, and when you do, you'll learn the information and strategies you need to turn things around for your child.

Many parents feel that their child's reading problem is beyond their control—that there is little if anything they can do to help. These parents believe that they are not up to the challenge of making a difference in their kid's reading behavior. Others feel that they are not sufficiently well educated themselves or that the family is just not "reading oriented." Some say it is the job of the school to fix the problem; they don't want to get involved. And still others realize that they could make a difference, but they are too busy with other commitments. Regardless of which group you belong to, it's time to stop listening to your fears and excuses and start helping your daughter or son learn the joy of reading. There's no better time to begin than right now.

About the Author

Wendy M. Williams, Ph.D., is a research faculty member in the Department of Psychology at Yale University. She received a B.A. degree in English and biology from Columbia University, a master's degree in anthropology from Yale University, and master's and Ph.D. degrees in psychology, also from Yale. Williams directed the joint Yale-Harvard Practical and Creative Intelligence for School Project, a research effort designed to help children succeed in school. She also heads a six-year study of practical aspects of success at leadership. Williams is the author or coauthor of scholarly articles on education and leadership, two books on effective teaching published by HarperCollins, a book on developing creativity published by the Association for Supervision and Curriculum Development, and a book on effective leadership to be published by Harcourt Brace. She is currently working on an educational psychology textbook, also being published by HarperCollins.

People say that life is the thing, but I prefer reading.
—LOGAN PEARSALL SMITH

Don't read science fiction books. It'll look bad if you die in bed with one on the nightstand. Always read stuff that will make you look good if you die in the middle of the night.
—P. J. O'ROURKE

The man who does not read good books has no advantage over the man who can't read them.
—MARK TWAIN

CHAPTER ONE

THE VICTIM OF BENIGN NEGLECT: ASHLEY'S STORY

When we read too fast or too slowly, we understand nothing.
—BLAISE PASCAL

Magazines all too frequently lead to books and should be regarded by the prudent as the heavy petting of literature.
—FRAN LEBOWITZ

Ashley sat in her room staring at the short story she was supposed to finish for her seventh-grade English class tomorrow. *The words looked pretty on the page,* she thought. Ashley swallowed and made an effort to continue, but her thoughts kept drifting to other, more interesting things... the school dance this Friday night, her current heartthrob Robby, school vacation week next month. As these thoughts filled her mind, she began to feel drowsy and bored.

In the kitchen, the family's housekeeper and baby-sitter, Donna, was on the telephone, as usual. Donna was a sort of zookeeper-warden whose job was to keep the house from falling apart and keep thirteen-year-old Ashley clean and fed. Aside from these duties, every

9

other one of Donna's brain cells was devoted to her social life—or, more appropriately, her sex life, since that was all she ever thought about. Ashley's knowledge base on the topic was impressive, and she owed it all to Donna. Predictably, with the exception of an occasional romance novel with a near-X-rated picture on the cover, Donna didn't have much time for reading.

Ashley's parents weren't around much. Her mother, Patricia, worked twelve-hour days as head administrator at a local hospital. Her father, Charles, was a radiologist in the same hospital. His work schedule was not as demanding as his wife's, but his athletic schedule was daunting: squash, tennis, golf, running; he worked out at least two hours a day. Ashley had an older brother who was a junior at an Ivy League college. Their ten-year age difference meant that Ashley had grown up much like an only child, with parents a decade older than those of her friends.

Ashley was a nice kid; everyone liked her. She was cooperative and well behaved at school and at home. She wasn't a troublemaker. Unlike her older brother, James, whom everyone described as a "real pistol," Ashley was a quiet child who tried her best to get along. Some of the teachers at school remembered James—so much so that the mere mention of Ashley's surname made them groan. But, contrary to their expectations, Ashley was not cut from the same cloth as her brilliant but demanding sibling.

Ashley was awakened by the jolt of Donna's voice calling her for dinner: another Lean Cuisine. Donna felt it was essential for Ashley to keep her figure throughout adolescence; it was her most important asset, and, as Donna kept repeating, fat cells deposited during youth

are never lost in adulthood. Donna and Ashley sat
down, pushed the pile of mail out of the way, and dug
in, amid talk of the upcoming school dance and Ashley's prospects of landing a prestigious date. Donna was
concerned about a zit Ashley was developing and spent
fifteen minutes describing home remedies, cover-ups,
and the emotional trauma of her own facial flaws. She
promised to help Ashley apply concealing foundation
makeup Friday night before the dance. As always, Ashley was grateful for Donna's sage advice and direction
in the area of life that had mattered most to Ashley ever
since she hit puberty.

Back in her room, Ashley once again picked up the
short story. Although she knew most of the words, there
just didn't seem to be any point in plodding through it.
Why bother, she thought. Donna's conversation drifted
in from her station on the stool next to the kitchen
phone. Ashley closed the book and daydreamed about
the dance; then she opened her closet door and started
to plan her outfit. Two hours later, every garment Ashley owned was on the floor, but Donna insisted that
none represented the right look. Tomorrow, they'd go
to the mall. According to Donna, a "yesterday" look
would doom the evening—without something decent
to wear, there was no point in going to the dance at all.

At school the next day Ashley began dreading her afternoon English class, when the short story she was supposed to have finished would be discussed. She asked a
couple of friends to summarize its plot: What were the
characters' names? What happened to each of them?
What lessons did they learn? What was the moral of the
story? Ashley was keenly able to anticipate her teacher's

questions. Two of her friends had read the story, and they filled her in on the details. But it was confusing to remember it all without actually having read past page 1. To help lodge the facts firmly in her mind, Ashley kept repeating over and over the main story line the way her friends had described it. But her friends kept interrupting the boring exchange about the short story to ask Ashley about her plans for the next school play. They wanted to know if she would be trying out and, if so, for what role. Despite her shyness in most social situations, Ashley was a natural actress who blossomed before an audience. Her friends were envious of her physical beauty and her talent and poise on stage.

Lunch passed quickly, especially since Robby sat next to Ashley. Her girlfriends jumped up and left the table, laughing and making faces at her. Ashley felt numb from head to toe at the thought that she could actually reach out and touch Robby if she wanted to. She prayed that he'd sat there with the intention of asking her to the dance. They both stared at their tuna sub, chewing purposively, saying little, as their friends gawked from neighboring tables. Ashley was so nervous that she forgot everything she had rehearsed for English class. And Robby never did get around to asking her to the dance. She knew it was because he saw the zit she was sprouting; obviously, no boy with Robby's style would be caught dead with a pizza-faced date. The bell rang and Robby sprang up, leaving Ashley to slink into the rear of her English class, hoping to remain unnoticed and uncalled on for the next forty-five minutes.

Teachers always know which kids are trying to avoid recognition—the hunched shoulders and evasive downward glances give them away. Mrs. Fishman was no exception; she'd been at it a long time, and she was better than a Secret Service agent at locating deceptive faces. So of course she called on Ashley right away: "Who can tell me which character they identified with most in this story? Ashley? Which character reminded you most of yourself?"

Long pause. Ashley swallowed, staring down at the book, as though the answer might be penned in somewhere on the margin of the page. "Ummm, well, I guess Kathy . . . because, ummm, she is my age and she has to go to school."

Mrs. Fishman was not impressed. "All the children in the story go to school, Ashley, and they're all in seventh grade. I'm looking for a better reason, something about how the characters think about their lives, the types of problems they face—you know what I mean. Why specifically did you identify with Kathy?"

Long, long pause. Ashley exhaled, looked down, and said, "Actually, Mrs. Fishman, I didn't read the whole story."

"How much did you read?"

"Well, ummm, only the first few pages. I didn't have time to finish it."

Mrs. Fishman knew the answer before she heard it, but she was glad that Ashley had admitted the truth. "All right, Ashley. Perhaps you could speak with me after class for a few minutes. Does anyone else want to describe a character they identified with?" Four hands went up, and Ashley was off the hook—at least for the moment.

After class she approached Mrs. Fishman with an ache in her stomach that felt like she'd eaten an entire sausage pizza. Mrs. Fishman, sitting at her desk, looked tired. She cared about Ashley because she knew the girl was bright and thought she was a good kid. But Mrs. Fishman knew that Ashley had no discipline when it came to her reading assignments. And as you might expect, her writing wasn't stellar, either. Ashely was average to below average in performance—but with well-*above*-average ability. Mrs. Fishman thought it was a shame and wondered what the problem was. Ashley didn't seem self-conscious, nervous, or sheepish the way neglected or abused children seemed; she didn't fit the profile of a child from an alcoholic or abusive household. Mrs. Fishman knew that Ashley's parents were well-educated professionals who cared about her and provided a good home. Her parents always came to teacher meetings and seemed concerned about Ashley's future and her below-average reading ability. So why was Ashley performing so far below her ability?

Mrs. Fishman asked her some questions to try to determine the cause of her lagging performance. What did she do every day when she got home from school? When did she do her homework? Was anyone available to help her? Why did she perform so much better in math than in reading? How much time did she spend on her reading homework? Did she read for fun— comic books, fashion magazines, anything? Mrs. Fishman decided to call Ashley's parents and set up a meeting. The statewide performance assessments were in three months, and Ashley's score would determine which class she was placed in next year. Mrs. Fishman knew that a lot was at stake for Ashley, and she knew that Ashley's future opportunities (including which high school she could attend) would depend on her placing within one of the higher-level classes for eighth grade.

Across town, Ashley's mother, Patricia, sat at her desk feeling overwhelmed by the stack of insurance company queries and complaints she was reviewing. The times weren't exactly low-stress for administrators in the health-care community. Patricia had members of every camp on her case: Doctors were worried about the move toward socialized medicine, nurses were overworked and underpaid, patients were complaining about delays in treatment and cost-cutting measures, and the hospital's directors were anxious about the hospital's financial future. Patricia was at the center of it all—she heard everyone's complaints and concerns, and she was expected to make peace among partners in the system who distrusted and sometimes even loathed one another. She had had it with prima donna doctors, victim-mentality nurses and patients, and greedy investors.

Patricia's thoughts drifted to her parents' farm in upstate New York and the horse and dog-breeding business the family had kept alive for thirty years. She knew they had been through rough times, but she longed to trade her own frenetic lifestyle for theirs. No crime, no commuting, no poverty, no urban filth, no living in fear, no smog . . . and people actually got to spend time with one another, talking and working together as a family. Patricia smiled to herself, knowing she had traveled this road a thousand times without ever doing anything about it. She loved the vibrancy of her New York City life; she'd probably be bored silly in a town of eighteen hundred people. But whenever life began to overwhelm her, she focused on her past, and on the lifestyle her parents still managed to lead. She instinctively reached for the phone and called her parents' house. She got the answering machine again. *They're probably out training the horses*, she thought. She left a message asking about the family's plans for Easter Sunday, then hung up and forced herself to open the next folder.

At that moment Patricia's secretary buzzed her. "Your daughter's teacher is on the line." Patricia's stomach tightened with a familiar twinge. She knew exactly why Mrs. Fishman was calling—Ashley's reading problem, again. She knew that Mrs. Fishman cared, but she wished she'd just let up on the girl. Ashley was going through a normal phase for an adolescent—true, all she thought about was boys, but what else was there at age thirteen? She lifted the receiver, and heard Mrs. Fishman play the same old tape she had played three times earlier this school year: Ashley was very bright, she didn't read at anywhere near her grade level, and she should be reading well above it; Mrs. Fishman wondered whether the family couldn't help Ashley bolster her performance before the upcoming assessments. The lecture was getting really old as far as Patricia was concerned. Ashley was an adolescent whose life was filled with boys, clothes, music, and a fixation on her appearance. It wasn't as if Patricia could change the situation—her daughter was going through a stage that was entirely normal for a girl her age.

Patricia dropped the receiver and snapped her folder shut. *Just what I need*, she thought, *another parent-teacher conference*. She knew it was important, but she had already put in her time with parent-teacher conferences this semester. Plus, it was so hard getting her husband to take the time to go at 3:00 P.M., when Mrs. Fishman wanted to see them. The whole thing was such a hassle: running across town before the day's work was done, just to spend forty-five minutes talking about the same thing they had talked about during the last two conferences. She just didn't see the point. On her commute home, Patricia resigned herself to the conference and decided to present it to her husband in as upbeat a manner as possible. . . whatever it would take to avoid an argument about it.

Patricia turned the key in the door and smelled chicken lasagna fresh from the microwave (obviously Donna's low-fat version). Thank God for Donna, she thought. It was seven-thirty and Ashley had been fed and the kitchen was clean. Donna and Ashley were finishing their dinners in front of the television in the living room. Patricia felt fortunate to have a reliable person to take care of her daughter every afternoon. School got out at two-thirty, and Donna could be counted on to take Ashley places and make sure she ate a decent meal. By the time Patricia got home she was too exhausted to think about preparing dinner. She ate her main meal at lunchtime and was never hungry at night. Her husband didn't get home from the athletic club until around eight o'clock, and he was on a specialized super-low-fat training diet with nutritional supplements and what looked and smelled like the least appetizing food Patricia could imagine.

Just as she finished changing into her fleece outfit, her husband walked in. Biting her lip, she broke the news right away: "We've been asked to come in again and talk to Mrs. Fishman."

Charles sighed and sat down on the edge of the bed, unlacing his megaperformance athletic shoes. "But we just went!" he exclaimed with a look of total frustration.

"Actually, we went a month ago," Patricia explained, "and Mrs. Fishman said it's important for both of us to come again."

Charles looked down at the rug and there was a long pause. "She's certainly no James," he said slowly, and Patricia nodded in agreement. "I mean, she's a great kid, and I adore her to death, but sometimes I miss those conferences we used to be called in for!" They both laughed. "Remember the kind of trouble James used to get into? He was always pushing teachers to go faster than they wanted to . . . and by Ashley's age he was reading at the twelfth-grade level."

Patricia looked down. "Come to think of it, I remember being angry at the time," she said in defense of her daughter. "It's funny *now*, but you used to complain about what a pain in the ass James was."

"Yeah, I know," Charles said, shaking his head, "but now I only appreciate him more! What a kid he was. It's no surprise he's doing so well at Princeton."

Patricia and Charles looked at each other approvingly, as though they'd crafted James from raw granite. "But Ashley's really beginning to bloom," said Patricia. "She used to be so shy, but lately she's been coming out of her shell. We owe it all to Donna—we're so lucky she answered our ad. When she came for the interview she seemed kind of lonely, like her life needed a purpose . . . and Ashley was shy and introverted. But they've had a wonderful effect on each other; they're like best friends. It's done Ashley worlds of good." Charles agreed. The sound of laughter filtered in from the living room. "She's worth her weight in gold," Patricia added, as she flicked on their own television and sat down to an evening of PBS while Charles, nodding in enthusiastic agreement, studied this month's *Muscle and Fitness* magazine.

Books are . . . funny little portable pieces of thought.
—SUSAN SONTAG

The possession of a book becomes a substitute for reading it.
—ANTHONY BURGESS

THE PROBLEM

Ashley *was* a great kid, as everyone kept saying—Donna, Ashley's parents, Ashley's friends, and Ashley's teachers (like Mrs. Fishman). Actually, Ashley was sort of like a low-maintenance house plant: Water it once a month and it will survive and grow slowly. What was wrong with this picture? A lot. Often, kids like Ashley get short-changed, particularly if they are girls. Ashley's parents treated her with benign neglect. They had absolutely no idea what she was working on for school—even if it had meant winning the lottery they couldn't name a report she had written or a project she had done or a book she was supposed to have read. They were kind to Ashley, but only in a detached way. And Ashley certainly wasn't convinced that she had much to offer.

In truth, Patricia and Charles were much more interested in their own lives, and this fact was obvious to Ashley, who had grown up in the shadow of her successful older brother, James. It got to the point that she would actually cringe at the mention of his name. Ashley loved James very much—he was the only person she knew who talked to her seriously about interesting topics like science and politics—but she didn't love it when her parents talked about him, which they did daily. James had done everything sooner, earlier, better, and more successfully than Ashley. Her parents beamed when they described his list of accomplishments, which included not only academic achievements but medals for swimming and tennis and recognition for his community service and work with the blind. How could Ashley possibly compete with James? She reasoned that it was impossible, so why bother even trying? Her parents acted like James was the family star, while Ashley was just the child they had when they were pushing forty.

Patricia and Charles thought Ashley was a normal young girl, but they never would have accepted her passive attitude and quiet compliance had she been a boy. They would have assumed that something was wrong, probed to get at what it was, and insisted on the maintenance of high standards. In Ashley's case, however, lower standards were accepted: Her adolescent stage was blamed for everything, as though she couldn't possibly be expected to do more now that she was hormone ravaged. Patricia and Charles didn't consciously think in these terms—but their attitude was characteristic of the way girls often are treated, especially in families with successful older siblings. Ashley's quiet, docile, sweet nature only augmented everyone's desire to treat her like a sweet dumb nothing.

Then, there was Donna. Donna had come into Ashley's life when Ashley had begun feeling like a ship adrift with nowhere to toss anchor. James had left for college, and Ashley's world had gotten five sizes smaller. Donna filled the gap with a bang. Donna was fun, exciting, and full of life. Trouble was, Donna was not terribly bright, nor did she have habits or interests that were the best influence on Ashley. But Donna cared about Ashley—as long as Ashley cared about Donna's interests—and Ashley so badly needed the attention that she willingly adopted all of Donna's concerns and made them her own. Donna was twenty-six, a high-school graduate who had studied cosmetology and then found a scarcity of jobs applying makeup in the "go natural" era. She was reliable and a warm, kind person. She was a fine baby-sitter, but she was not the ideal person for Ashley to spend all her nonschool waking hours with, as Ashley's primary adult influence. Donna herself had hated homework, reading, and all things academic, and she was unintentionally transferring those feelings to Ashley.

The problem with Ashley was that she was a bright young woman on her way to nothing much. She didn't apply herself, didn't perform at the level her ability would predict, and didn't excel as she might have. Ashley's life was headed down a slope of superficiality at an age when a child's focus is very important to what she makes of herself later on. Everyone liked Ashley—except Ashley, that is. She didn't think much of her abilities, and she had turned to Donna for friendship and reassurance in areas as far removed from school as they could get. The biggest casualty was Ashley's reading, and the love of learning that often goes out the window when reading ceases. Ashley didn't see books as even remotely related to fun: Fun was what she and Donna had at the mall. Patricia and Charles actually had a far bigger problem on their hands than they realized. But the real trouble was that ultimately Ashley was going to be the one to pay the price.

In the march up to the heights of fame there comes a spot close to the summit in which man reads nothing but detective stories.
—HEYWOOD BROUN

LOSING STRATEGIES

There's no doubt about it—Ashley's parents had tried to help her with her reading problem. Let's look at the strategies they tried and consider why none of them worked. One night while discussing their most re-

cent parent-teacher conference over dinner at their favorite restaurant, Charles decided he had had just
about enough of the situation. "We know she has the
ability, if she'd only apply herself! These conferences
are a waste of our time! I think we should let her know
that *we* know she's just not making an effort!"

Patricia agreed, so later that night they summoned
Ashley to the dining table for a mini-inquisition. They
told her that she had to try harder to improve her
marks in reading, that reading was all-important and essential to her later school placement. And they stressed
several times that James had never had these types of
problems, stating sternly that they were tired of accept-
ing this behavior from Ashley. She'd just have to try
harder, they kept repeating, over and over and over. . .
As Ashley slunk back to her room, she bit her tongue to
keep from crying. She knew she was no James, and
from her perspective she already was trying her best to
improve her reading. She felt disappointing to her parents and to herself. She kept thinking, *The only person
who accepts me the way I am is Donna.*

Another strategy her parents tried a couple of
months later was to offer Ashley a cash reward for raising her performance in reading. They told her in an
upbeat way about the extra money she could earn and
the new seventy-five-dollar ripped and frayed designer
jeans she could buy. Given how concerned Ashley was
with her appearance, Charles and Patricia were convinced that the financial-incentive route was the way to
go. Unfortunately, it didn't work. Ashley already had
lots of clothes and a big allowance. Plus, she knew
they'd never had to bribe James, and she was sort of
angry at them for trying it with her. What she really
wanted was for her parents to take a sincere interest in

her education and her life. Money wasn't a good enough substitute for their honest attention.

The next losing strategy involved Donna. Deciding to enlist some help from the ranks, Ashley's parents told Donna secretly that they'd give her a hundred dollar bonus for any month in which there were no parent-teacher conferences about Ashley's reading problem and in which Ashley's English grades went up. Donna was psyched up big-time and planned exactly how she'd spend the money. She then set herself on a "motivate Ashley" mission: She asked Ashley about her English assignments and made her spend more time on them after school. So, the quality time Ashley enjoyed spending with Donna was being taken away—Donna was asking her to spend time alone reading while Donna talked on the telephone. That wasn't fair in Ashley's mind. Later, Ashley learned that her parents had put Donna up to the whole thing for money. As you can imagine, this discovery did not do wonders to help the situation. Ashley felt betrayed again and reacted by trying less and less with her reading assignments.

When this approach didn't work, Patricia and Charles encouraged Donna to become even more actively involved in Ashley's reading problem. They reasoned that Donna knew how to read so obviously she could help their daughter. Donna felt insecure at the request since she had never perceived herself as much of a brain. She skimmed a couple of the stories Ashley had been assigned, then sat nervously with the book open in front of her trying to get the main points of the stories across to Ashley. The usually smooth-talking Donna stuttered and spoke in a disjointed way as she tried to explain the stories' themes. She interrupted Ashley whenever Ashley tried to read aloud or ask a question, correcting Ashley so quickly and sharply that Ashley felt like an idiot. The experience was a disaster. Just because Donna was a responsible baby-sitter and a verbally well-endowed woman didn't mean that she was qualified to tutor a thirteen-year-old with a reading problem.

In fact, Donna was so embarrassed at how her limited educational background compared to that of Ashley's family that she became intensely nervous at the mere thought of helping Ashley. The bottom line here is that sitting down and helping a child with a reading problem is a good idea, but it's essential to consider who is doing the helping. A defensive or unpracticed person (especially an untrained tutor helping a child for money) may do more harm than good. Ashley felt uncomfortable being with Donna in this new context; she liked the old Donna who never talked about books. Donna was typical of many people who want to help a child with a reading problem but who lack the basic knowledge of how to do so, and Patricia and Charles weren't around to help.

Of course, Mrs. Fishman was also trying to help Ashley—she wasn't spending all that time calling Ashley's parents because she liked them! With some families, the parent-teacher conferences would have been a big help by alerting parents to the problems and showing them honest strategies for overcoming them. But Mrs. Fishman's suggestions fell on dead ears because every one of them involved spending attentive time with Ashley and becoming *truly involved* in her schoolwork—something Patricia and Charles were too exhausted even to contemplate. This experienced and dedicated teacher had a list of workable strategies as long as her arm. Too bad these parents couldn't see the wisdom in these suggestions. Failing to implement Mrs. Fishman's winning strategies, which were based on an in-depth appreciation of Ashley's situation, was another big losing strategy for this family.

Another unsuccessful but well-intentioned strategy Mom and Pop tried was to summon James to the rescue. They prepped him with all the details and solicited his help in getting Ashley on the reading bus. James loved Ashley and really cared about the problem—but he lived down at Princeton and just wasn't around much. James was a busy twenty-year-old with his own life. He did call Ashley and ask about her English class and her reading projects and book reports, but there wasn't enough contact between the two of them to make it work. Plus, he was almost never around in person. At thirteen, Ashley was too young to learn through a correspondence course or over the phone, and too undisciplined to police herself in response to James' pleas. But now she felt even worse about herself for failing to meet her brother's expectations. Now she wasn't just letting her parents down but James, too.

Another lightbulb-dimming strategy was Patricia's idea to make more time for reading by curtailing Ashley's involvement in what Patricia perceived as "inessential activities." She believed that Ashley's participation in the school drama group was taking too much time away from studying, so she discouraged Ashley from trying out for the new play. Ashley was crushed when her mother said the play wasn't worth her time: She'd always thought her parents were proud of her acting and singing, but now, suddenly, she realized they didn't care. This lowered Ashley's self-esteem another notch. Needless to say, Patricia's strategy did not exactly skyrocket Ashley's reading performance.

Patricia became exasperated as nothing seemed to work and took Ashley shopping one Saturday afternoon. While they tried on clothes, Patricia brought up the topic of succeeding in school, and all the doors that school success would open for Ashley. Ashley listened absentmindedly. She was far more concerned with how she looked in her all-gray waif outfit (too fat, she thought), and asked her mother whether she thought Ashley should try a new diet to slim down before the next school dance. Patricia blanched at the thought of her ninety-five-pound daughter dieting and ripped into her for even suggesting such a stupid idea, thus ending the heart-to-heart about the importance of succeeding in school. Ashley obviously had other priorities, and Patricia reasoned that time would be needed for Ashley to mature into a solid student who cared about succeeding in school the way James had.

The key to all of these losing strategies is that they were Band-Aid approaches: attempts by Patricia and Charles to engineer a quick fix when what was needed was a deeper-level attitude and behavior adjustment on everyone's part.

Where is human nature so weak as in the bookstore?
—HENRY WARD BEECHER

WINNING STRATEGIES

Do you think Patricia was right? Was Ashley normal? Were her reading problems typical of an adolescent girl growing into a young woman with better things to worry about than the theme of redemption in Charles Dickens? Would Ashley outgrow her reading problems on her own? Was Mrs. Fishman overreacting? What would *you* do if Ashley were your daughter?

Whether Ashley might on her own and over time deal with some of her scholastic problems is almost irrelevant. The middle-school years are a critical period when skills are developed that prepare a child for adult careers and experiences. Unlike music class or woodshop, reading skills are central to all academic work, and these skills must be built progressively from grade to grade. Waiting around for Ashley to outgrow her adolescent obsessions wouldn't work. By the time she did become a serious student (if ever), it would be too late and she would have lost too much ground relative to the other bright students. Plus, Ashley's personality and interests were being formed and influenced in an undesirable direction, and there is no reason to expect that she would spontaneously trade in fashion, makeup, and soap operas for book reports, science projects, and visits to bookstores. The key is that reading and the joy of learning are *habits* children must *develop*. The enjoyment of reading is not usually a spontaneous discovery in a world where there are so many competing influences on children's time, most of which take a lot less active self-directed energy than reading. Ashley needs help—but she sure isn't getting it. What strategies would be winners for Ashley, her teachers, her parents, and everyone else who cares about her?

The single biggest winning strategy for this family involves a change in perspective on the part of Ashley's parents. They are up to their eyeballs in professional and personal commitments and lead a hectic life in a frenetic city. And they have a fabulously successful first-born who they think walks on water. Much of their behavior toward Ashley reeks of the "but we've already *raised* our kid" syndrome: the battle cry of overworked, overtired, and overcommitted parents with a successful child or children and another offspring who needs more help. Ashley's parents loved her, but they didn't have time for her. They never sat and read to her and never talked about her reading and schoolwork except to hear a quick report on her last grade. Patricia and Charles were immersed in *themselves*; their daughter received less attention than many people's pets.

Ashley's low self-esteem and her feelings of inferiority in comparison to James were a logical outgrowth of her parents' attitudes. Ashley felt insignificant to her folks, and, in reality, she was. She was the victim not of intentional or malicious mistreatment, but rather of benign neglect. Ashley's reading problem was serious, but it was only one of many signs that something was wrong inside this young woman. Without a change in the parents' attitudes, Ashley's reading problem would be simply the first in a long list of school and outside-of-school problems in the years to come.

The key to every winning strategy for Ashley is for Patricia and Charles to increase their energy and caring level and *deliver the goods* for their daughter. This means spending real time with her, talking to her, listening to her, and reading alongside her. There is no substitute for parental time spent with children: Surrogates can't completely replace parents, and those pep talks and quick words of wisdom that parents place so much confidence in don't do the trick either. Let's consider how this attitude realignment translates into specific winning strategies that will help Ashley.

One major way in which Patricia and Charles could help their daughter is by reading *themselves* in the living room instead of holing up in their bedroom watching

PBS. Patricia and Charles read a lot, but not out where Ashley sees them. By moving their act into the living room instead of hibernating every evening, these parents would get more in touch with their daughter's reading, schoolwork, and life. They would actually get to know her as a person by spending the type of quality time they used to spend with James—and they might even find that Ashley's just as special as their wonder boy. Maybe one reason why all Ashley talks about is fashion and boys is that her primary after-school adult contact talks about nothing else. But Charles and Patricia can change this trend by moving their butts out into the living room. There's no need for Donna to be spending every evening with Ashley after her parents arrive home. One of them could even make an effort to get home a bit earlier each day to have more time to spend with their daughter.

Donna may be a good baby-sitter, but she shouldn't spend so much time with Ashley. A weekly trip to a bookstore or library with one of her parents would be a worthwhile substitute for one of her weekly trips to the mall with Donna. Charles and Patricia should also consider alternatives for their daughter's after-school time from two-thirty to six-thirty—activities that will involve her in an active and positive way, such as the drama group, music or art lessons, or an athletic activity. A bright and capable girl like Ashley should not be spending every afternoon involved in passive activities, whether at a mall or in front of a soap opera on TV.

Another big winning strategy would involve a bit of detective work on the part of Ashley's parents, who are surely up to the task. Ashley has some skills; she just feels that all her skills are overshadowed by James's stellar track record. Patricia and Charles must ask themselves carefully and thoughtfully what skills Ashley has in areas related to academics that James wasn't medaled for. The closer the skill is to reading, or the more it involves some element of reading, the better. For example, Ashley acted in the school play last fall, and by all reports she did a very good job. She sang the musical numbers with grace. Her lines were memorized perfectly and spoken without a hitch. Best of all, James never made it big in school plays; this was something Ashley could do that James did not excel at.

Ashley's folks could focus on this skill of their daughter's and *encourage* it (instead of labeling it a drain on reading time and therefore discouraging it)—possibly enrolling her in a special drama group after school and buying her books about acting and the theater and copies of plays she might like. The school plays she was in were fine, but she was talented and capable of benefiting from additional training. This outside-of-school activity would build Ashley's self-confidence and help her see herself for once as being good at something that James never accomplished; good enough, in fact, to become a member of a young theater group. James could be called on the telephone and warned about Ashley's new and developing skill—and he could be asked to make this Ashley's special area of competence. Patricia and Charles might even work up the enthusiasm and chisel an opening out of their schedule in order to take Ashley to a couple of Broadway plays, thus showing her that they do have time for her and her interests.

The nice thing about Ashley's ability in this area is that it involves reading—plays, scripts, lines, books, you name it . . . but Ashley won't even realize she's reading because it's not in the same domain as her schoolwork.

Her parents could show some excitement about her interest, and Ashley could meet people who spend more time buried in plays than Donna does on the telephone. Although helping kids like Ashley overcome reading problems doesn't have to include acting in a school play or membership in a drama group, it should include a focus on an area that involves *reading* without creating tension and anxiety about *grades in reading* for school.

Another idea likely to pay off is to get subscriptions for Ashley to a bunch of teen magazines with articles about fashion, makeup, and teen issues, thus capitalizing on the fact that she's a hormone-ravaged teenager. She's talking about the stuff all afternoon with Donna—why not get her to actually *read* the stuff too? Similarly, Charles and Patricia could buy a few books on fashion and makeup. Ashley would appreciate the show of interest in something that really matters to her at age thirteen—and she would learn that we get *information* and *valuable ideas* from the printed word (not just boring plots about kids she doesn't know).

The point in giving her teen magazines is that they require reading without seeming to Ashley like reading with a capital *R* (i.e., the reading she is assigned in school). After all the misdirected attempts to help her, Ashley gets as tight as a crow's beak at the thought of her reading problem. She becomes defensive and stubborn and unwilling to bend; you might, too, in her position. Ashley has some sound reasons for feeling dumped on by her parents. The truth is, they don't think Ashley's as bright or as special as James was at that age. But they love her, and with a little bit of effort they could discover her own unique skills and gifts. Which brings us to the next bright idea—which is really more of a suggestion for Charles and Patricia than for Ashley.

Having had a handsome and successful son (whom they thought would be their only child), Charles and Patricia felt fulfilled in their parental roles. James was everything anyone could ask for in a kid. They had planned to have him, and they think he's as wonderful as chocolate. Where does this leave Ashley? She was *not* planned: She didn't fit in with her parents' lives when she made her appearance nine months after their summer in Europe. The moral of this story is that Patricia and Charles must recognize their daughter's needs and her sensitivity to being compared constantly to James the megabrother. It might be nice for her parents to stop praising James for everything and start taking a more balanced view of their daughter and her significant gifts. They do care about her; they've just been selfish. If they want Ashley to reach her potential as a young woman, they need to start caring about who she is rather than simply comparing her to James. Plus, James wasn't always so terrific—and it might help once in a while to remind Ashley of that fact, especially when she's feeling lost in his shadow. James has the benefits of ten years' experience over Ashley and the softening effect of time when Patricia and Charles look back on his debacles.

Another workable idea is for the family to plan a vacation for next summer—and trust Ashley to suggest activities and details, which she could find in brochures and guidebooks that her parents could leave on the coffee table. Again, the focus of these winning strategies is on deemphasizing academic success (especially as compared with James's) and emphasizing reading for fun, valuable information, and other good things reading brings, like being able to memorize lines for a play or knowing there's a great coral reef in Central America. Treating Ashley like a bright and special kid with unique talents wouldn't hurt either.

An essential element of the winning recipe for Ashley involves her parents' attitudes, which must shift. They think she's normal; even if they're right and she is a typical adolescent, her situation is certainly not auspicious. True, many girls Ashley's age obsess about clothes, looks, and boys—but they are also studying and getting excited about sports, science, music, whatever. Ashley belongs in this group, but getting her into it depends on her parents' recognition that she deserves and is capable of more—and on seeing that it is their responsibility to provide Ashley with more instead of letting her off the hook. There are no quick fixes for problems like Ashley's. Her parents have to take a look in the mirror and work on what's wrong with their attitude, behavior, and perspective before they can expect real change. But with a few changes in attitude and their daily routine, Ashley and her parents will see real gains in her reading grades and real increases in reading for fun, because Ashley will learn to see herself as a competent individual who *can* and *should* succeed at reading.

Books think for me.
—*CHARLES LAMB*

MORALS OF ASHLEY'S STORY

How to Get and Keep Kids Reading

• If your reluctant reader is a girl, ask yourself if you would be more concerned about her reading if she were a boy. If the answer is "yes", you are doing your daughter no favor by holding her to a lower standard.

• If you resent the time spent in parent-teacher conferences, ask yourself whether you've been giving enough time and attention to your child's reading problem. Your child cannot solve the problem alone.

• If the adults in the home are wrapped up in their own lives, the child may not be getting enough attention and support—especially with academic activities.

• Examine the quality of your child care. Is it adequate? Is your child getting the support she needs with reading and schoolwork? If the answer is "probably not," explore other options.

• Never relax standards for younger children compared to older ones just because you lack the energy and zeal you once had. Expect just as much from the baby of the family, and help her achieve it.

• Accept your child's interests even if they bore you or you think they're foolish, and buy or borrow books and magazines related to these interests for your child.

• Never dismiss reading problems as "normal." They may be common, but each child with a reading problem needs immediate and ongoing help. Reading problems almost never disappear by themselves!

• Don't expect your child's school and teachers to solve the reading problem without your help. Your involvement is necessary regardless of how good the school is.

• Counteract your child's tendency to feel depressed about the reading problem by playing up her biggest assets and skills, and by encouraging her to read about things she's good at (to *link* reading to subjects she likes).

• You should be able to describe your child's last two book reports and school projects in detail. If you can't, you are too detached from her schoolwork and reading, and it's time to get more involved.

• Read where your child can see you, and describe interesting facts you've learned from reading to try to engage your child in a discussion that shows the value of information gained from books. Choose topics your child will find interesting.

• Enlist the help of people your child admires to encourage her reading and applaud her successes.

CHAPTER TWO

THE COMPUTER JOCK: BEN'S STORY

Whoever would know himself, let him open a book.
—JEAN PAULHAN

The limits of my language mean the limits of my world.
—LUDWIG WITTGENSTEIN

Ben's mother called him for the third time to come downstairs for dinner. It was a good thing she hadn't put the food on the plate, or it would be ice cold by now, Sandy thought. Were all sixteen-year-olds as self-absorbed as this? "Where are you?" she yelled, stomping upstairs to locate her son.

At Ben's door she was greeted by the sound of smoothly clicking keys; Ben was at the computer again. Sandy pushed the door open but Ben didn't even notice—he was staring into the computer screen, the room lights dim, his face reflected on the screen amid the confusing mass of numbers and incomprehensible code. Incomprehensible to Sandy, that is; Ben knew exactly what was going on.

When Sandy screamed, *"DINNER!"* Ben turned around, surprised to see her standing there. "Hi, Mom! What's up?"

Sandy exhaled long and hard. "Ben, your dinner has been ready for twenty minutes. I've been calling and calling. What on earth do you do up here hour after hour?"

"Sorry. I lost track of time," Ben said as he stood up, stretched, and followed his mother downstairs.

Ben's younger brothers Michael and Jason had already finished their dinner. Ben sat down and Sandy delivered his plate onto the table with a definitive slam, indicating (in case there was any doubt) that she was not pleased. "How's school going? How did you do on the English test? Did you get your grade on the composition you wrote last week? Did you talk to Ms. Ritter about retaking the vocabulary test?" Sandy pelted Ben with questions—more than most eleventh graders could answer with their mouths full.

Although it was tough to find time to chew, he tried to eat while answering. "Why are you so worried, Mom? My grades are fine. I want to be a computer scientist anyway, and the only courses I have trouble with are courses that don't matter. Who cares what I get in English? A *B*-minus is fine! All my other grades are *A*s and *A*-minuses. Why are you always on my back? I spend every free minute I have on schoolwork—it's like a full-time job! What ever happened to letting me be a teenager?"

Ben finished his meal as fast as he could considering the third degree he was undergoing. He felt a tightness in his stomach that seemed to appear whenever he talked to his mother . . . or, more appropriately, when *she* talked to *him*, since the communication was decidedly one way. Ben answered the questions as quickly as he could, volunteering absolutely no additional information beyond the minimum needed to placate Sandy. Then he thanked his mom for dinner and asked to be excused.

"Why don't you go into the family room and spend some time with your brothers?" Sandy asked. "They never see you! They both look up to you so much . . . You know, Jason has been having trouble with math lately; maybe you could help him with his homework for a while."

Ben acquiesced. In truth he didn't mind helping his brother—it was just that he never seemed to have any personal time. Ben wished he could have a couple of hours to himself to play around with his new computer program or call Mandy, a girl he liked at school. But instead he spent an hour helping Jason with math, then Mike wanted some help with *his* homework, then just as Ben was heading upstairs his mother needed the garbage taken out, then the dog needed to be walked. . . and by then it was 10:30 P.M. and Ben was exhausted, so he just went to bed.

When the alarm rang at 6:30 A.M., Ben didn't feel like crawling out from beneath the warm covers. It was 12 degrees outside and the ground was covered with snow. Ben looked out the window, assessing the magnitude of the snowfall. He had recently learned how to downhill ski and was eager to go again. *Maybe I could ask Mandy,* he thought. Ben ran for the bathroom to beat his brothers, showered, and dressed. By 7:30 he had eaten breakfast, packed his stuff, and was out the door. This morning he was meeting with the other kids on the math team to discuss strategy for the upcoming meet, where they would compete against their arch rivals from the high school across town. Ben was psyched up—he really liked being on the math team. Mr. Delgado, the teacher in charge, had told Ben that he was gifted and had suggested that he take advanced placement courses in math, physics, and computer science to start getting college-level training. Mr. Delgado was encouraging Ben to think big about college, which Ben liked; but with his mother's constant pressuring, there was a part of Ben that wanted nothing more than to enjoy himself like any other sixteen-year-old.

The math team meeting went well—Mandy was there and Ben sat next to her, where he could smell her hair and think about kissing her. Mandy certainly took Ben's mind off of math, although she was one of the team's top performers. Mr. Delgado got the team thinking about the upcoming challenge from their rivals: How could they anticipate the other team's questions? What could they do to prepare? How about a mock meet after school on Thursday? Ben took notes hurriedly so that he would remember to review some important formulas before the meet. As the first-period bell rang, Mandy took Ben's hand and asked him what he was doing on Saturday. Ben's heart felt like it would beat right out of his chest. Then Mandy asked him to a party at her house, and Ben was on cloud nine.

The spell was shattered when Ben got to English class. He really disliked his English teacher, Ms. Ritter, who seemed to live to make his life miserable. Ms. Ritter always picked on Ben and his friends. She acted like she had a personal vendetta against the kids on the math and computer teams; she thought they should be spending more time on reading and writing instead of losing themselves in technology at age fifteen or sixteen. Predictably, she drilled Ben almost from the moment he sat down. "Ben—what can you tell me about character development in *Macbeth*? What was Shakespeare trying to do with Duncan in the opening speech? What did he mean when he wrote, 'So foul and fair a day I have not seen.' " Ben groaned almost audibly in response. Ms. Ritter's eyes narrowed. "Did you read the play, Ben? Or are you spending all your time working on the computer as usual? Your English assignments are important, too—you can't get through life on technical ability alone!" Ben sank into his seat, humiliated. Why should he even bother to answer the questions, he thought. There was no point. Ms. Ritter already hated him. Plus, he never "got" Shakespeare; he couldn't understand why kids his age had to read that stuff. It was meaningless. Yes, he had tried to read *Macbeth*, but after a while he found that he was just mouthing the words without even processing them. He hated English class and was thankful it would be over by nine-thirty so he could get on with his day.

As Ms. Ritter attacked her next victim, Ben tuned out, writing some computer code in the margin of his English notes. He looked at his watch, counting the minutes left in the class. As his mind drifted, Ms. Ritter brought him back to life. "Ben, was there anything you liked about *Macbeth*? Or was it all boring to you?"

Ben hesitated. "Uhhh . . . I liked the character of Lady Macbeth." His friends snickered, and one of them whispered that it was just like Ben to like a Shakespearean play because of its female characters.

Ms. Ritter sat down looking tense and angry. "What specifically did you like about Lady Macbeth?"

"Well, I liked the way she kept trying to wash the imaginary blood off her hands." When Ms. Ritter asked

"Why?", Ben looked down. "I don't know what you're getting at, Ms. Ritter. I read the play."

"Yes, I can see that, Ben, or at least you read the Monarch Notes!" Ben stiffened and shook his head. *Why bother with this?* he thought. Ms. Ritter circled away like a buzzard, but Ben feared she'd be back. He hoped the bell would ring before she pounced on him again.

At home that night, Ben sighed and opened his copy of *Macbeth*. There was a report due next week: five to eight pages about the juxtaposition of good and bad imagery in what Ms. Ritter called "Shakespeare's greatest play." Ben ached physically at the thought of writing the paper. *What a heinous task,* he thought. *Why should I have to do this? What difference does it make?* Just then his mother called him downstairs with a list of chores to do. For once, Ben was grateful for the excuse to get up from his desk—he would much rather clean out the garage than write a meaningless report about a stupid play that took place hundreds of years ago.

When Ben got downstairs he started to tell his mother all about the math meet and Mandy and the party on Saturday. He was talking fast, all bubbly and excited, as he helped to put away the groceries. But Sandy wasn't really listening—she was waiting for Ben to tell her about his most recent English grade. Finally, frustrated, she interrupted him. "Ben! Be quiet for a second. I've got a lot on my mind. What did you get on the English test? How did you do on your composition this week?"

Ben paused. "Mom, I've been telling you all about what's happened at school this week! Haven't you been listening?"

"I know you've been talking, Ben, but you haven't

been telling me what I want to hear. I know you like the math team, and this girl sounds nice, but what matters are your grades. Now, how did you do on the test in English?"

Ben felt totally dejected. He looked down, put down the can of tuna fish he was holding, and went to his room. His mother rolled her eyes, thinking how unreasonable Ben had become.

Sandy changed into her nightgown and eased her tired feet into warm wool socks. She was exhausted. This was nothing new; she was always exhausted. Life was a daily challenge. She'd never thought she could end up this way. Then she smiled to herself, thinking how ironic it was. They'd been such a happy family . . . or at least she had thought so. Sandy still didn't understand what had gone wrong. She was lonely; she desperately needed someone to talk to, but Ben was too busy (as usual), and all her friends had families of their own and 9:00 P.M. wasn't the best time to call. So she turned on the TV in her bedroom and settled back on the bed.

Sandy was stressed out a lot of the time, and she knew she was being hard on Ben. But in all fairness, she was doing her best. Ben's father, Alan, had left her three years ago to marry someone half his age. He'd announced he was leaving and had left the same day. No offer to attend counseling, no attempt to work things out, no time for the boys to get used to living without their father. He just up and left and started his life over, and for Sandy, raising three energetic, bright sons on her own was a minute-by-minute challenge. They lived in a nice house, and Alan kept up with the child support, but that was about all he did. Oh, there were the visits on major holidays, but three boys need more from their father than an occasional chat. Plus, Alan's new wife was pregnant, and his priorities were with her and the new family he was beginning. By this point Sandy had gotten over the intense anger she'd lived with for the first year; now she felt resentment, she felt victimized, and she felt tired.

Sandy worried a lot, too. She so wanted Ben to succeed brilliantly at school, to set the best example for his younger brothers—and to show Alan, their two families, and the world how well the boys were turning out despite the fact that their dad had abandoned them. It meant more to Sandy than she could admit, and she knew she pressured Ben the most by expecting him to carry the burden as the eldest. But she reasoned that Ben was a young adult and should start getting used to pressure—life was full of pressure, and a bright young man would have to deal with it from every corner. Ben was too old to be doing sloppy work in school and fooling around with the math team and computer club and other nonsense when he should be worrying about his grades. And Ben was too young to be getting serious about a girl. Sandy depended on Ben to help out—she was a single parent raising three children, and she needed his support on a daily basis. She believed that the experience of taking care of things would prepare Ben for adult life; or at least it would encourage him to wait before starting a family of his own!

What worried Sandy the most was Ben's not caring about his English class, his reading and writing assignments, his book reports, and all the work he was supposed to do that was unrelated to math, computers, science, and other technical subjects. She thought that Ben was far too one-sided. That stuff was a fun diversion, she reasoned, but it would never get him into college. He had to do well on the SATs, and his reading performance was weak. She decided that she'd have to get tougher on him and make him spend more time on reading. Sandy leaned back and closed her eyes as the plot of her weekly nighttime soap lost its grip on her. Five minutes later, she was snoring, the television was still on.

That same night, Ms. Joan Ritter was grading English essays. When she got to Ben's she stopped to put on a pot of coffee. She suspected this paper would be a tough one to grade—and she was right. It infuriated Joan that Ben and his techno-dweeb friends took their English and language-arts work so lightly. She thought that reading fine literature was one of the greatest joys in life—and that writing a solid essay was one of the greatest marks of a keen mind. And here were those snotty kids, mocking her, not even trying their best, not caring if they got *B*-minuses and *C*s. It was disgusting.

Joan poured a tall mug of black coffee and sat down to Ben's essay. Of course it was beautifully word processed, but it was filled with grammatical errors, unclear sentences, and generally sloppy writing. He made some good points, but he made them in such a convoluted way that Joan could barely discern what he meant. Another *B*-minus or *C*-plus job. She hated the way Ben failed to apply himself. He had never once given her class an effort. Other students with half of Ben's ability were doing better than he because they tried and worked at it and gave it the time it deserved. But Ben just rushed through, handing in his first draft more often than not. (And it read like a first draft; teachers can always tell.)

Another thing that drove Joan crazy was the other

teachers' and the principal's attitudes toward her and her complaints about the new generation of technology-awed students. It was a personal mission of hers to keep reading and writing as central goals of education, as she felt they should be. She sensed the school's pulling back from its commitment to basic educational values in order to devote more time and money to technology and the hard sciences, and she resented the trend. Kids today couldn't even write a decent sentence. They read Monarch Notes or Cliff Notes instead of the books. They watched TV or played computer games instead of reading. The brightest kids were being encouraged to put all their energy into science, math, and computers. Their parents supported it, the school supported it, the other teachers supported it—but it was not in the students' best interest. Joan was angry, as usual. *That must be why they go around calling me a bitch,* she thought, *because I want to uphold basic standards.*

Just last month there had been a big altercation with a couple of parents. At mid term, Joan had legitimately flunked one girl, Sarah, who she thought was quite bright and capable. Sarah didn't put any time into her English assignments, and it showed. Joan had warned her three or four times, but when the midterm bookreport was handed in two weeks late, Joan was infuriated. The report was filled with inaccuracies about the book, poor sentences, and bad spelling, and generally was a disaster. Joan talked to a couple of Sarah's other teachers and was shocked to learn that her work in her science, math, and computer classes was first rate: another techno-dweeb who put all her energy into only what she liked and thought was important. Joan's anger intensified when she learned that Sarah was very bright and capable of so much more than she had produced for Joan's class. So she gave her an *F*, just as much to stir things up with everyone—the principal, other teachers, students, and parents—as to punish Sarah herself.

Joan achieved her goal of causing a ruckus: Sarah's parents complained and came into school. They met with the principal and took the position that Ms. Ritter was basically a mean-spirited individual who had singled out their daughter for attack. All the college applications that would be completed the following year called for a transcript, and the *F* would stand out and severely limit Sarah's chances for getting into the types of schools she was applying to, and which she deserved to attend. The principal was furious, and the other teachers became agitated: Why was Joan causing so much trouble? The girl was a bright student—the *F* was clearly not justified; a C, maybe, if the work was poor. In any case, the other teachers believed that Sarah should have been given the opportunity to rewrite the paper for a better grade. But Joan used the situation as a forum for her personal concerns about the decay of the educational system. She really let it rip. She attacked everyone around her, making more than several enemies in the process. The incident was resolved by the principal, who overrode Joan's grade and replaced it with a *C*. Joan was left feeling humiliated and angry and used, and less willing than ever before to back down on the issue of the central importance of reading and writing in education.

This story about Sarah's experience shows that as Joan read Ben's paper, she brought a lot more to the situation than simply a critical eye: She brought a reservoir of anger and resentment. Admittedly, she was stubborn and difficult, but her position was not without merit. She really cared about providing a quality education and felt sick at the declining pattern of standards. She had lots of energy, and she used it to pursue her self-styled mission to teach the kids in her high school the skills they needed to take on the world outside of school.

As Joan finished her cup of coffee she also finished Ben's essay. Her comments filled the last page. She tried to show Ben exactly where he had gone wrong, even rewriting his opening sentences and explaining exactly how she would have written some parts differently to better make key points. She spent almost two hours on Ben's paper. Shaking her head and rubbing the back of her neck, she pushed the paper into the graded pile and headed for bed.

All the glory of the world would be buried in oblivion, unless God had provided mortals with the remedy of books.
—RICHARD DE BURY

The habit of reading is the only enjoyment in which there is no alloy; it lasts when all other pleasures fade.
—ANTHONY TROLLOPE

THE PROBLEM

Ben certainly did have a problem, and it was not only with Joan Ritter. He was a gifted student who belonged at a top college—but bad grades from Ms. Ritter and other English teachers and bad scores on the SAT English section would definitely keep him from realizing his dream. Ben did so well in his technical courses and received so much encouragement and support from the teachers of those courses and from the math and computer team coaches that he lost touch with the fact that reading and writing were important. The school didn't help much, either. It encouraged Ben's focus, and the principal did not take steps to ensure that basic standards were maintained across the entire curriculum. Ben was getting *A*s in the courses he loved, so why worry about his *B*-minus or *C*-plus in English? He reasoned that no one is perfect; plus, his average was still high enough to get him into a good college. What Ben didn't realize was that poor performance in reading and writing would affect him throughout his school career and later life—and that colleges would not look past poor grades in English and poor scores in reading comprehension and vocabulary, because top colleges know that to succeed in their competitive environments, students must be able to read and write effectively.

Then there was Ben's mother, Sandy. She had been through a tough time: Losing your husband of twenty years to a twenty-four-year-old bimbo is not a pleasant experience. Sandy had a demanding career as a real estate agent, the pressures of an uneven income, and a heartfelt desire to give the best to her sons. She knew that each of her children was capable of growing up to be successful, and she saw Ben as the example setter, the one carrying the ball, the one taking the lead and setting the tone for Mike and Jason. And Sandy was lonely, too. Between her job and her kids, she didn't have time for much of a social life. She worked in a bustling real estate office and spent her days surrounded by people—clients, lawyers, and other agents—but she had few friends to whom she could really open up. So Sandy did what she thought was only logical, turning to Ben for friendship and support.

The trouble was that Ben was sixteen years old. Sandy needed things Ben couldn't provide—he was wrapped up in his own life, and although he wanted to help his mom, he was still a kid trying to grow up in his own way. When Sandy placed demand upon demand on Ben, she made him feel that nothing he ever accomplished was good enough. She didn't place much value on what Ben was good at—often because she didn't *understand* what Ben was good at, and because Ben's skills reminded her of her delightful ex-husband, who was an electrical engineer and who had turned Ben on to all that technical stuff in the first place. So Sandy shut down when Ben tried to tell her about what excited him, and this made Ben feel like yesterday's news. His performance on the math team didn't matter—all Sandy kept harping on were his grades in English class, which were the last things on his mind.

Sandy also expected Ben to carry too much of the burden with his younger brothers. He was not a live-in tutor, but often this was how he felt. He wanted his own independent life, and he wanted to spend more time with Mandy after school. But Sandy expected him to come home and watch over his siblings, and even do marketing and housework so that when Sandy walked in the door exhausted after a ten-hour day of showing the same house ten times, she could get dinner on the table quickly. Ben felt a lot of pressure—he was being treated like a husband rather than a son. Plus, he didn't know how to be his mom's friend (although she obviously needed one), because whenever he tried to open up to her about what mattered to him, she pulled the "I'm your mother" thing and started lecturing him. All she seemed to want was for Ben to listen to and repeat how bad things were for her; she didn't interact with him as her equal, because he was her son, but she wanted to tell him everything she should have been sharing with a same-aged friend and confidante. Ben didn't want to hear what a slime his father was for the ten-thousandth time. He wanted to discuss what a bitch Ms. Ritter was, but when he tried, Sandy always took Ms. Ritter's side and sent Ben to his room to do more English homework.

What it all came down to was that Ben was a teenager ripe with possibilities who might easily self-destruct instead of making it in the world. His priorities were a bit off center, but this was understandable considering the situation. He had an extremely difficult English teacher, but her points were not wrong, even if she did have the tact of a pit bull. Ben never really *read* books— and he couldn't write a decent paragraph if it was a note revealing his location as a hostage. Aside from Ms. Ritter, the school didn't seem to care. His mother cared, but she didn't know the winning strategies that could help Ben. So, Ben was headed for a definite near-miss; a real tragedy, considering everything he had to offer. What should his mother have done to help, and what did she actually do instead?

Sartor Resartus is simply unreadable, and for me that always sort of spoils a book.
—*HARRY S TRUMAN*

LOSING STRATEGIES

All the key players in Ben's life had tried to do what they thought was best to help Ben overcome his deficit in reading and writing skills. Too bad their efforts were misguided. And often, misguided efforts end up making the situation even worse!

First, there was Ben's mother. Sandy was so distressed at the thought of Ben's doing poorly on the SAT verbal section that she nearly got a migraine headache. She saw the SATs as the portal to Ben's future—the limit on everything he would become, and the great decider of where he would go to college. It may sound ridiculous to think this way, but Sandy was largely correct. The SATs are overused in admissions decisions, holding many bright teenagers back from good colleges, but for now this is the world we're stuck with, and Ben would be the big loser. So, with the SAT specter hanging over her head, Sandy enrolled Ben in a Saturday-morning preparatory course designed to raise his score by 200 points. In fact, his math score was already 750, so Sandy hoped the verbal score would show the whole jump! A prep course sounds like a good idea, so what went wrong? Well, true to form, Sandy didn't discuss the situation first with Ben—she just signed him up. Yes, she talked to (or rather *at*) him a lot, but she never discussed issues with him to hear his side and work out a common solution. After paying for the course, Sandy dropped some brochures on Ben's desk and left him a note ordering him to mark off Saturday mornings starting in a couple of weeks.

Ben hit the ceiling; he felt like he was being treated like a three-year-old. "Since when is it fair to just *announce* what I'm going to do instead of discussing the situation with me?" he screamed. He was really worked up, but not because he didn't want to attend the SAT prep session; actually, he realized the wisdom in getting help on the verbal section because he wanted to get into a good college. What infuriated Ben was that his Saturday mornings were already spoken for—that was when his math-team meets were held this term. He couldn't simply blow off the math team and Mr. Delgado to attend a course that was also given on Sunday mornings and Tuesday afternoons!

When he confronted his mother and suggested that they change the day of the course, she snapped back, saying, "I don't want you away from the family for the whole morning every Sunday, because that's family time." Every Sunday she would make a big breakfast for the boys before running off to show some clients the house of their dreams. Ben would usually watch to make sure no disasters happened until Sandy got back around midafternoon. So the Sunday morning SAT course was out of the question, as was the Tuesday night after-school course, because she wanted Ben to come home and do chores and make sure no horrors were happening with his brothers (a common theme in a house with three boys). Ben was infuriated at Sandy's suggestion that he abandon the math team—he thought she should be more flexible about Sundays or Tuesdays. They fought until Sandy started to get a headache and sent Ben to his room.

Sandy's other brilliant idea had to do with Mr. Delgado. She knew that Ben admired the coach of the math and computer teams, so she stopped by to talk to Mr. Delgado after school one day. Sandy said she wanted help in realigning Ben's priorities and asked Mr. Delgado to redirect her son. She explained that Ben spent all his time on technical subjects like math, physics, and science, and she wanted him to spend more time on book reports and reading. She suggested that it would be in her son's best interest in the long run if Mr. Delgado asked Ben to take a leave of absence from the math team. That way, he could attend the Saturday morning sessions of the SAT course. Plus, Ben just cared too damn much about the math team, and some time away from it and Mandy would help him hone his concentration and focus on what was really important in life.

Mr. Delgado was shocked at Sandy's idea. As a kid, he himself had been like Ben, enjoying the focus on the more technical end of the spectrum; besides, he needed Ben on the team. Mr. Delgado tried to reason with Sandy, pointing out that Ben had made a commitment to the team and that it was a bad idea to teach him that once something else comes along, commitments don't matter. He said that Ben was truly gifted, and that although reading and writing were very important, Ben should not abandon his gifts in other areas. Then he suggested the Sunday morning SAT class, which we know Sandy's opinion of! It came down to a basic disagreement between Sandy and Mr. Delgado, and little progress was made. However, Mr. Delgado agreed to do what he could to encourage Ben to try harder in his other classes.

But that wasn't the end of the "visit Delgado and convince him" story. When Sandy told Ben that she thought Mr. Delgado was letting the kids down by using them for his own interests as team coach, instead of encouraging them to do what was best for them, Ben became even more furious. Why had Sandy gone and made waves? he demanded. Ben felt violated again because Mr. Delgado meant a lot to him, and here his mother was suggesting that he give up the math team. When this disaster simmered down, Ben cared less than ever before about attending any SAT course, and more than ever before about staying on the math team. Sandy was well-intentioned, but she blew it.

As Sandy's distress about Ben's grades in English mounted, she realized that in Joan Ritter, she had a compatriot; the teacher felt even more ardently that reading and writing should be the center of the curriculum. When Sandy and Joan got together it was like identical twins meeting after being separated at birth. They got each other totally worked up and agreed that getting Ben on the reading and writing bus was the best thing either of them could do for him. Sandy gave Joan ideas on how to persuade Ben—mostly things about how math and computers weren't that important but reading was, and specific details from Ben's life that illustrated why he should spend more time on reading, like how his English grades had kept him from winning an outstanding-student award last year. Joan agreed to put more pressure on Ben, demanding that he read one extra Shakespearean play and write one extra book report this month to force him to realign his priorities. Sandy agreed to support Joan with sanctions at home. Together, they believed they could get Ben to spend his prime time on work for English class instead of on math, computers, and science stuff.

Another lightbulb-dimming idea of Sandy's was to link, unfairly and punitively, Ben's permission to see Mandy and his friends to his performance in English class. Sandy decided that it would be wise to restrict Ben's social activities until his English grade was at least a B-plus. So she told Ben that he couldn't attend any parties until Ms. Ritter agreed and his English grades showed the improvement. Curtailing Ben's social time might have been a defensible position had he been spending lots of time socializing and no time on school-work, but that was hardly the case—Sandy had cut off all social activities rather than limit them somewhat. Ben now felt like a victim in a police state. He did laundry, went marketing, took care of his brothers and the dog, and did his best in school. How could his mother possibly think it fair to forbid him to go to parties! Ben couldn't believe it; he simply said, "I'm going anyway," and left the room—to which Sandy responded, "Not in this lifetime!" as Ben slammed his door.

The net result of all of these losing strategies was that Ben took the hit, winding up an even bigger loser at reading and writing than before. He became more and more angry about his mother's pushy interventions, and he thought Ms. Ritter was Frankenstein's second experiment. The thought of not being able to see Mandy because he had to read *The Tempest* made him feel like he was going to lose his lunch. Ben's response was to redouble his efforts in math, science, and computer classes and tune out even more in English. His papers got sloppier and less engaging; his attention in English class wandered; and *The Complete Shakespeare* on CD-ROM was not at the top of his birthday gift list. As far as the SATs were concerned, Ben figured he'd just do his best without any course to help him prepare for the verbal section. Trouble was, he never had the time to work on developing his ability in this area: All his time was spent on his technical-course work, the math and computer clubs, Mandy, and taking care of the shopping, cleaning, and Mike and Jason. This kid was headed down the road to pressure-induced illness. Some winning strategies were certainly in order!

If a book is worth reading, it is worth buying.
—JOHN RUSKIN

WINNING STRATEGIES

All those brain cells must have been capable of reasonable success with Shakespeare, even if Ben couldn't possibly see how. A bright, competent, responsible teenager like Ben could obviously do more than he was doing. Many parents would gladly have traded their pot-smoking slobs for such an nice kid. Too bad Sandy didn't realize how lucky she was; she spent all her time worrying to herself and complaining to Ben. So the first in the set of winning strategies involves Sandy's behavior, which is truly at the root of much of Ben's problem.

Although always well intentioned, Sandy has been making several egregious errors in her interactions with Ben. As is so often the case in such situations, there were many aspects of her behavior that had nothing to do with her son's poor performance in English class—but reading and writing were what she had fixated on, and she wouldn't let up. The first and most important winning strategy for Sandy is to start treating Ben consistently (not like a ten-year-old one second and a husband the next), and to start caring about who Ben is as a person. True, her slimeball ex-husband, Alan, had gotten Ben started on all the computer stuff, but Ben was legitimately interested in it and good at it. This was not Alan's fault; Ben had inherited his father's ability in technical areas. Sandy's rejection of Ben's focus on technical material was partly an outgrowth of her hatred of her ex-husband: She wanted Ben to be more like her and less like his father.

But where did this leave Ben? He had loved this stuff since he was seven years old, when he and his dad would play with computers and play chess and talk about all sorts of things Sandy didn't understand. The key is that Ben defines himself as a technical expert—it's *who he is* and it's what he wants to spend the rest of his life doing. Maybe at sixteen he shouldn't be deciding his whole future, but at least he has some drive and ambition, unlike the typical kid his age whose parents and teachers complain "cares about nothing." Ben really cares; his mother doesn't and she shows it. To make any progress whatsoever with Ben, Sandy must respect who he is today and show some interest in *his* interests. The kid is a star performer on the math team, but Sandy has refused to listen to this kind of talk, so when Ben comes home from a meet, he has no one there to share his successes with. It's no wonder that he admires Mr. Delgado—the coach cares about Ben's successes and supports him in his efforts. So the first winning strategy is for Sandy to take a reality pill and accept her son the way he is. But how does she communicate this attitude shift to Ben?

To start out, she should halt all attempts to control his academic performance, at least for the time being. She should continue to ask Ben regularly about what happened in school, but let him choose the topics. If he fails to mention his score on an English test, Sandy shouldn't bring it up. If he talks about the math team, she should legitimately try to get interested in all that mumbo-jumbo by asking Ben to explain some of it to her. If he talks about Mandy and an upcoming dance, she should tell Ben a story about when she was his age and liked Norbert Nuthouse from across town . . . anything, as long as it isn't contentious. The goal is to let Ben set the pace, and to act, look, and *be* interested in what he has to say. Giving Ben some breathing room and showing him he's valuable and worthwhile just as he is is a great first step.

The next winning strategy is for Sandy to support Ben in what he's good at—to talk up his successes to her friends and to Ben's, to call and thank Mr. Delgado for providing such an important resource for her son, and to attend a couple of math meets even it if means missing a client or two. Ben is a star in his own way, and he needs a mother who realizes it. At the same time, Sandy should deal honestly with her need for friendship and intimacy, and not simply dump those raw needs on her son and expect him to meet them. By forcing Ben to fulfill the roles of son and husband and friend, Sandy is placing too much pressure on him and on their relationship. Maybe Sandy should join a support group for single parents where she can discuss some of her issues openly with a sympathetic audience. Or perhaps she should take a course at night in cooking or basket weaving or genetically engineering a new slime mold that reminds her of Alan—it doesn't really matter what she does, as long as it gets her out of the house and into contact with new people who are not co-workers or clients. What Sandy needs is to let off steam and find her identity away from her kids and her job. It would make her a better parent and a better real estate agent.

As Sandy gets a grip on the realities of the situation, she may begin to see that Joan Ritter is not the Joan of Arc she once thought. Sandy should try to see Ms. Ritter through her son's eyes. Ben does not usually have trouble with teachers, but Joan has been a problem since the Wednesday after Labor Day. Maybe Sandy could learn to see that although this teacher means well, she is harsh and even brutal to the kids and shows them no respect as individual human beings. Every time Sandy takes Joan's side, she pushes her son farther away because he rightfully feels unfairly treated by Joan. So Sandy's behavior ends up causing the exact opposite reaction from what she had hoped—once again, her son reads less and cares less about his performance in English class.

But the fact is that Ben will have to deal with Ms. Ritter at least until June, so it would be wise if Sandy could help the situation instead of making it fester. One winning strategy is for Sandy to have a heart-to-heart with Ben, beginning by telling him that she truly wants to hear how Joan treats Ben in class. Sandy should listen honestly and openly to the answer, quelling her ever-present need to jump in and interrupt, and then tell him what he should have thought or done, or generally control his feelings. If Sandy can shut up and listen, maybe she and Ben can come to terms with the fact that Joan is difficult, but Ben is stuck with her for the year. Plus, Joan gives the grades that could hold back Ben's progress, so pulling away and ignoring her class is a sure route to disaster. If Ben and Sandy talk it out, Sandy can ask him what he thinks they should do about the situation. In fact, this is one of the biggest winning strategies of all, never more relevant than in this situation: Sandy has to shut up, stop second guessing her kid, listen, and really work on a solution *together* with her son.

With someone like Joan Ritter, a visit from Sandy could help a lot to ease tensions, as long as Sandy plays it right. If she goes to the school in a complaining, angry mood, speaks to Joan and the principal about what they're doing wrong to her son, and stomps out, Sandy will be passed off as another petulant parent who can't see that her kid's a brat. Sure, the principal knows Joan's difficult, but if all Sandy does is try to make trouble, he won't have much of an option except to try to calm her and wait until she leaves to throw darts at her picture. About all Sandy will accomplish by using her usual pushy antics at school is to guarantee more business for the real estate firm across town.

But if she plays it cool, acknowledges that her son is wrapped up in the technical side of things, and suggests a few specific strategies to improve the situation, some ground may be gained. As Joan's handling of the Sarah incident shows, she is a temperamental teacher with a fragile ego who tends to lash out when threatened. She's also more than a bit stubborn. Sandy can work around these weaknesses of Joan's by approaching her in the right frame of mind, and Sandy can use her people-smarts to smooth things over. First, Joan needs to be heard and validated, and Sandy can do this. Second, Joan really does want kids to read, and Sandy can make a few suggestions to help get the pages turning. For example, Ms. Ritter could assign open book reports once in a while, where kids choose their own books to read (maybe even books about the development of computers, great hackers of the past twenty years, and so on). Ms. Ritter could also allow kids to write compositions and essays about topics that are important to them, instead of topics relating just to Shakespeare and the other books they have been assigned to read (even if some kids write about why they love hacking, it's still writing, it's communication, and it's a learning experience for the kids). Sandy might also ask Ms. Ritter to agree to wait a week (or longer if she can stand it) before calling on anyone whose hand is not raised, just to give the kids who never volunteer a chance to raise their hand before being called on. Joan may be totally closed to all of these suggestions, but Sandy can try. And Sandy can tell Ben that she tried honestly to help. If nothing else works, Sandy can remind Ben that he'll be out of Ritter purgatory soon.

Then there's the treadmill situation at home. Sandy has to lighten up on all the requirements here. As it now stands, Ben wouldn't have time to read and enjoy a book if he wanted to. The environment is not exactly ripe for reading. What specific steps can Sandy take to change this? First, she can buy some books that Ben— not *Sandy*, but *Ben*—would like, those same types of books Ben's father used to read all the time. She could leave the books lying around where Ben will see them. Second, Sandy could subscribe to a few computer magazines for Ben. It might not be *As You Like It*, but it's reading Ben will become enthusiastic about, because it will concern a topic he's interested in. Third, Sandy could so some reading herself in the living room after dinner as her kids do their homework. It never hurts to read once in a while so your kids don't see you as someone who never takes her own advice. Fourth, Sandy could enroll in a night class in word processing or some other computer-oriented skill she could use at work. Then, when she buys the two or three books the teacher recommends, she can make sure that Ben sees her reading them. (A wise mother might even ask her son to explain or teach a couple of things to her.)

There are other, smaller steps Sandy could take that

would make a big difference to Ben. One of these is to compromise, allowing some give and take. For example, if Ben will take the SAT course, Sandy will agree to let him take it on Sunday mornings. Letting him take the SAT prep course on Sunday mornings is actually a good idea—it's only for six weeks, and there will be more pancakes for Sandy and Jason and Michael. Instead of criticizing Ben for wanting to take the course on Sunday, Sandy should compliment him on his willingness to give up the only morning of the week he has off. And instead of attacking Ben about his time commitments to the math team, Sandy might acknowledge the importance of the team to Ben and her admiration of his maturity and commitment. Mr. Delgado admires Ben very much—it's time that his mother started showing Ben some respect, too.

The key lesson for parents like Sandy is to back off, cool down, stop nagging, and start really listening to their kids. Ben was doing so much so well. He needed to be told he was special, but his mother just complained all the time. The more Ben felt unappreciated, the closer he became to Mr. Delgado and other people who rewarded him with well-deserved praise, and the less he cared about reading and writing. An honest discussion with Ben could open a few doors. And Mr. Delgado could appropriately be enlisted for help here—Sandy could ask him to help her make the point to Ben that he deserves to attend a great college, but that gaining admittance depends on good SATs and good grades in English. Hearing this from someone he respects might make a difference to Ben.

Some free time would also make a difference—instead of all the babysitting and housework, some time just to sit on his bed and read computer magazines. Household chores are important to teach children responsibility, but Sandy should make clear, in advance, both the nature of the tasks and the amount of time necessary to complete them. Ben must be allowed to fit his chores into his schedule in a way that works for him. Sandy's habit of springing tasks on Ben is unfair—she should let him plan his household duties and be fair and consistent about assigning them. Perhaps Sandy and Ben could sit together and write up a list; if they do, Sandy must honor this agreement. By giving Ben the opportunity to plan his time, he will be better able to take control of his schedule, and he will be ensured of some free time. Learning to enjoy reading requires two ingredients: Number one is the *time*, number two is the *right book*, and both numbers depend on a less-pressured environment. The funny thing is that one of the reasons why Ben is so adept with computers is that he learned about them before it was a class requirement—he played with computers in his free time because he liked doing it, not to get some grade. But reading had never played this role in his life. Reading was always what he had to do to get the grade and get into the next class or, now, the right college. No wonder Ben never picked up a book for fun!

Sandy could also help out when it comes to Ben's next paper assignment. If the topic is at least somewhat open, Sandy could take Ben to a bookstore and show him some books about computer-related topics or stories he might be interested in. She could suggest he try writing about what he loves; maybe this would light him up. Sandy could also tell Mr. Delgado about some of the books, and see if he might suggest some page-turners to the members of the math and computer teams. Maybe getting away from Ms. Ritter and the heavy weight of her demands would allow Ben and the others to discover the joys of reading in a more positive context. And while she's at it, Sandy could make sure Ben has time left over for Mandy. After all, he's a normal sixteen-year-old boy.

In literature as in love, we are astonished at what is chosen by others.
—ANDRE MAUROIS

MORALS OF BEN'S STORY

How to Get and Keep Kids Reading

• If you've been pushing hard and nagging your child, try easing up. Let your child talk about what he *is* good at; don't always steer the conversation to reading or English class or subjects your child is having problems with.

• Don't take the side of your child's teacher against your child—instead, listen to your child's perceptions about the teacher. Next, ask your child to take the teacher's position and explain it to you (if he can!). Work with your child to achieve a common-ground understanding of the situation.

• Don't make major decisions about how to solve your child's reading problem without first discussing these ideas with your child and hearing his side.

• Don't burden your child with so many chores and

activities that he doesn't have the time or opportunity to read.

• Discuss with your child the role of reading performance in attaining goals he seeks. Offer a few examples of how poor reading performance might mean missing out on something he values.

• Show *interest* in subjects your child *is* good in—ask about these subjects; get details; look, act, and *be* interested.

• Don't constantly set up older children as examples for younger ones—allow older kids to feel it's okay to make mistakes and fail, as long as they learn from these experiences.

• Encourage reading by having reading material around that will interest your child, even if the material does not seem worth reading to you.

• Read about a subject your child likes, then share your new knowledge with your child. Ask your child to explain or teach you more about the subject.

• Limit older children's responsibility for younger children's academic growth. Helping siblings is one thing, but it's not healthy for a child to feel overly responsible for tutoring and mentoring younger siblings.

• Remember to acknowledge good performance in subjects other than reading.

• Visit difficult teachers to hear their side of the story about your child's reading problem. Make them feel heard and validate their position to soothe bad feelings, then enlist their support, stressing common goals.

• Acknowledge any reading effort or progress, regardless of how small—show that you know your child is trying. Don't postpone praise until large gains are made.

• Enlist the help of teachers or other adults your child admires—have them suggest reading materials and related activities to your child.

• If your child doesn't remind you of yourself, accept that this is who he is. He may not share your interests or your love of reading. Work with his needs and goals to nudge him to read.

CHAPTER THREE

THE OVERSCHEDULED AND OVERCOMMITTED CHILD: LAURA'S STORY

Reading is to the mind what exercise is to the body.
—SIR RICHARD STEELE

Anyone who knows how to read has it in their power to magnify themselves, to multiply the ways in which they exist, to make their life full, significant, and interesting.
—ALDOUS HUXLEY

Nine-year-old Laura waited nervously at the school's side door for her sister Linda. It was 2:45 and Laura could hear her mother's car idling outside. *Where is she,* Laura wondered, beginning to shift her weight from side to side. Just then Linda came running down the stairs, coat half on, backpack in hand. "We're going to be late!" Laura barked, pushing open the door and leading Linda by the hand to Mom's Livery Service. "Hi, guys!" their mother, Carol, said, turning around to give each daughter a kiss before pulling away from the curb. "How was your day?" Both girls started talking as fast as they could at exactly the same time, outdecibelling each other and even the car horns and street noise as they traveled down the highway. Carol was taking the kids to a gymnastics lesson at a special gym across town, something the girls had been doing at least three times a week since kindergarten. As soon as Carol had pulled up the driveway, the girls jumped out and ran to the locker room to change clothes. Carol grabbed a pile of paperwork and headed in behind them.

Laura and Linda looked like twins, although they were a year apart in age. They were the type of kids even grinches and old bachelors smile at: cute, happy, and endlessly giggling, with matching hairdos and outfits. Laura had just turned nine, and Linda had just turned eight. Laura was in third grade and Linda was in second in a rural-suburban area about a hundred miles outside of a major midwestern city. Their mother worked as a department supervisor in a local clothing store. At thirty, Carol looked more like the girls' older sister than their mother. She put all her time, effort, and soul into her children; they were the center of her life.

As Laura and Linda worked through their routines with the rest of the gymnasts, Carol watched from the spectator seats while reading an order manifest and double checking it against a receiving log. She had to keep up with her work somehow, which was tough considering how much time the girls took up. Not that Carol resented a minute of it—in fact, she'd turned down a promotion last month because it would have cut even further into her time with them. "They're only young once," she'd told her manager, who had nodded in understanding and assured her that there would be other promotions when her children were a bit older. So, Carol squeezed a full work week out of her time with her children by being at the store when they were in school, and then working evening and weekend shifts when the girls were visiting their father or friends or occasionally having a baby-sitter.

The girls' father, Todd, worked as a manager in a manufacturing company. He and Carol had met in high school and married the summer after graduation. The girls came along soon after; and soon after that, Carol and Todd realized they had nothing in common except their high-school yearbook and their children. The couple had divorced with considerably less animosity than had many of their friends, and Todd had committed to remain in the same town so that he could see his children frequently, which he did. Carol and Todd maintained a positive relationship, thus sparing their daughters the ill effects of a bitter divorce. It paid off: The kids were well adjusted and happy. Their parents adored them and spent all of their free time and their last after-tax dollars to ensure that the girls were brought up correctly.

A week in the life of Laura and Linda was a little like riding a merry-go-round. The girls were up at dawn, when they packed lunches and extra clothes, with the help of Carol, who would then drive them to school by 7:00 A.M. There was a bus at 8:00, but the girls had gymnastics and diving practice in the morning because they were on the school team. After a forty-five-minute workout, the girls showered, changed, and started their academic day at 8:15. A half hour for lunch at 11:30 was the only down time the girls had all day. At 2:45, Carol picked them up and took them to the day's after-school activity: special gymnastics and diving lessons at the nearby gym, competitive gymnastics and diving meets, piano lessons once a week, and art class once a week. Plus, the girls had friends they wanted to see, and this was usually fitted in after practice or class, by around

5:00 P.M. Sometimes the girls would go to their friends' houses for dinner; other days, Carol would feed one or both of her kids as well as one or more of someone else's. It would have been an exhausting schedule for an adult, much less a little kid, but the girls were used to it. It was certainly exhausting for Carol, who felt like a chauffeur. "If only I could get paid for my effort and hard work in taking care of these kids," she would remark, "I'd be a millionaire!"

Two nights a week, Todd took over at 5:00 P.M. and Carol worked the evening shift. He supported the girls' activities because he had been a competitive swimmer and diver himself, winning his first medals at the age of seven. Todd took the girls most weekends, too, when Carol put in two more eight-hour shifts. Todd and Carol saw eye-to-eye on how to raise their kids most of the time; both wanted their children to have the opportunities to develop their natural athletic and artistic talents fully. Todd had been an athlete, so the girls were going to be athletes. Carol was artistic—she had always loved to sing, and her hobbies included sculpting and ceramics—so the girls would be given lessons in music and art to keep them from becoming one-sided. How did the girls feel about all this? They loved it. They were gifted athletes, they both sang and played the piano well, and they had never known any other kind of life. They were two little kids with a much fuller schedule than mine (and probably yours).

Laura and Linda came running over to their mother at the end of practice, dressed in matching hot-pink leotards. "Can we have spaghetti for dinner? Can we please have spaghetti..."chanted Linda, tugging on her mother's sleeve.

Carol packed up her paperwork and put on her

jacket. "We've had spaghetti twice this week," she said. "How about chili?"

"Okay," Laura answered, as the sisters trailed their mother out to the car.

They stopped at the grocery store, did the marketing, and got home around five-thirty. Carol started dinner and told Laura to do her homework. When dinner was ready but the girls were nowhere in sight, she walked into their bedroom and found them both asleep with the television on. She shook them gently and said, "*Dinner!*" which worked up a little enthusiasm. By the time the girls were at the kitchen table they were ravenous.

As Carol cleared the table, she reminded Laura to do her homework. She was especially concerned about this because Laura's grade in reading on her last report card had gone down a bit—she had gotten an 80, when she used to get 85s and 90s. Linda, on the other hand, was only in second grade—she had no homework to do, so she was allowed to watch TV in the bedroom. But Laura had a book to finish for class: *The Ancient Egyptians*, which was mostly pictures of pyramids and tombs and mummies. There was almost no text in the book, and what there was was fairly low level. Although Laura loved the illustrations, and sat pointing excitedly at the various temples and artifacts, she was having a lot of trouble getting through the text. Carol knew that Laura's teacher, Mrs. Pratt, liked Laura, and she hoped Mrs. Pratt would be willing to help Laura. As Laura sat struggling with a caption about preparation for mummification and the afterlife, Carol thought to herself, *She needs more practice, that's all. She just doesn't give it enough time. These vocabulary words were tough for me.* She decided to send a note to Mrs. Pratt asking for a meeting one morning next week when she took the girls to school—and she hoped Mrs. Pratt wouldn't mind coming in at 7 o'clock!

Mrs. Pratt wasn't thrilled with the request, but she agreed to the meeting because she was a dedicated teacher who wanted to help. In fact, Mrs. Pratt was more concerned about Laura's slower reading than Carol was; as a teacher, Mrs. Pratt saw Laura in comparison to the other students in the class, whose skills were beginning to pass Laura's. The process had been gradual—Laura had fallen behind a little bit at a time—but now the cumulative effect was starting to have a significant impact on her ability to keep up and follow along in class.

Carol didn't realize the extent of the problem. Since Laura had only just turned nine, her mother thought her reading difficulties meant she was a little slow in developing the ability to read alone. But from Mrs. Pratt's point of view, Laura was in need of direct and immediate help. She knew from experience that a bright child like Laura would find her education and self-esteem compromised if her reading ability was allowed to slip. To get Laura reading along with the class the way she had in first and second grade, Ms. Pratt planned to suggest that Carol enroll Laura in a reading-enrichment program at the local library two or three afternoons a week. The program was designed to get kids more excited about reading so they would spend more time at it. By practicing more, their reading levels would get back on track, and even in some cases surpass the levels of their classmates.

The morning of their meeting, Mrs. Pratt got to her classroom at 7:00 A.M. sharp. She yawned as she turned up the heat and opened the shades. Just then Carol knocked on the door and entered. The girls were at their early-morning gymnastics practice, so it was a perfect opportunity for a teacher-parent discussion.

"I'm worried about Laura," Carol began. "She doesn't seem to be reading as well as she should be. Lately the books you have assigned her have been too difficult for her—she struggles with some of the words. She tries, but I don't think she's improved much since the start of the school year."

"I know," answered Mrs. Pratt, "and I've just received her reading standardized test scores. She's always been a good reader, but her scores slipped this year." Mrs. Pratt went on to detail at length the types of problems Laura was having and the solutions she recommended.

Carol listened intently, looking concerned. But when the teacher got to the part about the after-school reading enrichment program, Carol tensed and shook her head. "That's impossible," she said, "The girls have things to do every day right after school." She went on to describe the activities Laura and Linda participated in—diving and gymnastics, piano, art class, and time with their father.

Mrs. Pratt was amazed at the girls' schedule. "And it's now seven-ten in the morning and they're at practice, you said—right? When do they wake up? What time do they finally get home from school? When do they have a chance to do homework? When do they *sleep*?" Mrs. Pratt asked. Carol explained what a typical week was like, assuring Mrs. Pratt that all the girls' needs were met.

"I know they're well taken care of," Mrs. Pratt responded, "but they are doing too much for such young children. No wonder Laura is beginning to fall behind. She's very bright, but she doesn't get any time to practice at home like the other kids. As the years go on, time spent on homework becomes more and more important. Laura kept up until this year because there was no homework—but now she needs time to work after school, and next year she'll need even more."

Carol felt assaulted by Mrs. Pratt's comments. "But the girls *love* all their activities. They're talented divers and gymnasts, they love piano and singing, and they're both so artistic! Those things are important, too; life isn't just school and academics."

"I know that," answered Mrs. Pratt, "but you're going a bit overboard! Your daughters don't even have time to themselves on weekends—they're too busy at practice or competitions or recitals or playing with their father. When do they have time just to be kids?"

Carol looked stunned. She got up, thanked Mrs. Pratt for her time, and said she'd think about her recommendations. Walking down the hallway, she reflected on the discussion. She couldn't understand why Mrs. Pratt had attacked her parenting skills. Carol's daughters were by all accounts well-adjusted, successful, happy, beautiful children. They had never been troublemakers, and all their teachers liked them. Their extracurricular activities were absolutely essential. Carol couldn't understand why Laura's reading problems couldn't be dealt with within the school day, perhaps during lunch period. Laura could eat her sandwich and then have a remedial reading class or something, Carol reasoned. Further, she already got enough exercise, so she didn't need the free play time with the other kids. As she opened her car door, Carol made a mental note to call Mrs. Pratt and ask whether this solution would be possible.

That night, Carol called her ex-husband to hear his

reaction to Mrs. Pratt's suggestions. Todd went ballistic at the mention of curtailing their daughters' athletic and other after-school activities. He was forking over most of his discretionary income so his girls would have the best possible start in life. For Laura to miss diving or piano just to go to a library reading hour seemed ridiculous. "She can read anytime!" Todd said. "Why does it have to be from three to four on school days? That's crazy! She's got better things to do in those hours after school than read! Why don't you just make more time for Laura to work on reading after dinner?"

"She's pretty tired by then, Todd," Carol answered, "but I can try to work with her every night that I have the girls. Can you do the same?"

"Sure," Todd answered. "We'll have to fit it in somewhere. We can also make sure she works on her reading for a couple of hours on Saturday afternoons while the rest of us watch a video or something."

"That's a good idea—she won't be as tired then," Carol answered.

She then went to find Laura to explain the new family rule about reading time. But by then it was eight-thirty and both girls were asleep, still dressed in their warm-down outfits.

The next day in school, Mrs. Pratt made it a point to ask Laura about her schedule (even though she already knew). She wanted to hear how it seemed from Laura's point of view. Laura described her activities and said how much she loved gymnastics, diving, piano, art class, singing, and her father and mother. Mrs. Pratt smiled. "But, Laura, when do you work on reading? Do you have enough time to do the homework I assign? When will you be able to do your book report project that everyone in the class is working on? It's supposed to be done by next week."

Laura opened her mouth, then closed it and looked down. "I don't know," she answered.

"Laura, I think it's important for you to spend time after school on reading. Can you do that? Can you promise me you'll spend some time every day when you get home?"

"Yes, Mrs. Pratt," Laura answered.

As Laura returned to her seat and the subtraction exercises the class was doing, Mrs. Pratt wondered how Laura was going to be able to keep up with her academic demands now and in the future. True, Laura had won several awards at diving and gymnastics competitions, but Mrs. Pratt knew that the chances of her becoming an Olympic gymnast or diver were pretty slim. And Laura's chances of becoming a professional musician weren't any higher than anyone else's her age: She wasn't a child prodigy who would end up playing Carnegie Hall by age ten. Laura was very talented at the activities she participated in, but she clearly was not the one-in-ten-million type who becomes a superstar. Maybe she would ultimately become a musician or artist, but at age nine she needed to learn how to read well and independently.

Mrs. Pratt knew what is was like to be in Laura's parents' shoes. Neither Todd nor Carol had had the benefit of the advantages they were providing their children. Todd had been an athlete and Carol had taken art classes, but they hadn't done with their lives everything they might have wanted to. Their children were the most important part of their lives, and they wanted them to have every chance—the best possible start—to become their best. These feelings were natural, and

Mrs. Pratt had met many parents who felt this way over her twenty years of teaching. But the real problem today was Laura and her slipping reading level. Reading ability underlies success at almost every other academic endeavor, and Mrs. Pratt knew there was no higher priority than getting Laura's reading performance up to the desired level.

Laura continued working on the subtraction exercises in her math workbook. She was worried about all this talk about her reading. She knew her mother had met with Mrs. Pratt, and she wondered if she was in trouble or something. She couldn't imagine what she'd done wrong—it seemed like everything was going well with her and her parents. Yeah, she'd kicked her sister during a fight last weekend, but Linda had started it by stealing the last Superfrosted cookie, which was clearly Laura's. She was especially worried about the way everyone was talking about her after-school commitments. She hated the thought of missing out on any of her practices, meets, lessons, or classes. She hoped they wouldn't make her miss anything, nor did she understand why everyone was worrying all of a sudden. Then Laura started worrying herself, but not about reading; she started to obsess about the statewide gymnastics meet coming up that weekend.

By Friday night Laura was having quite a bit of anxiety about the meet. The best schools in the state were sending their best performers to the competition. This was Laura's big moment. Todd and Carol were more excited and nervous than Laura ten times over. Carol washed Laura's team leotard twice to make sure it was perfectly clean. She made a special trip to the store to buy a hair ribbon and plastic tie-back in the exact same shade as the leotard. And Todd kept psyching Laura up by talking about the psychology of competition every time he saw his daughter during the week before the meet. He brought out some of his own awards, won when he was Laura's age, just to show her what she had to look forward to and what was possible. Both parents went a bit overboard, and Laura was paying the price with a dry mouth, shaky hands, and absolutely no appetite. Not surprisingly, that week did not include time for Laura's reading: She was too busy being nervous and practicing her routine. Her parents reasoned that there would be plenty of time for reading practice next week.

When Laura awoke on Saturday morning at six o'clock, she had a pain in her stomach from a combination of nerves and not eating the night before. She managed to force down some hot oatmeal, then the doorbell rang and the girls and Carol ran out to meet Todd in the minivan. They had a one-hundred-twenty mile drive ahead of them and the meet started promptly at ten o'clock, by which time Laura had to be dressed and ready to perform. Laura didn't usually get carsick, but combined with her sick stomach upon awakening, the car's motion didn't help. She turned green and had to ask her dad to pull over twice so she could vomit. "It's natural," Todd said to Carol, who looked concerned. "I always got nervous before big meets." When the family got to the gym in the city where the competition was being held, Laura was overwhelmed: It was huge, there were hundreds of people there, and she had never performed in a place like this. She hugged her mother as they walked into the locker room. Meanwhile, Todd took Linda to buy some food and find their seats.

Laura changed her clothes, drank some water, and

went running across the room to her coach the minute she came into view. The coach calmed her and told her to join the team, which was assembling across the room. Carol kissed Laura, fixed her hair for the fourth time, and headed out to sit with Todd, feeling sick to her stomach and tense. She and Todd were white-knuckled as Laura's team marched in; they were so nervous that neither could speak as they watched their little girl approach the mat for her routine. In fact, the parents were probably more nervous than Laura by this point, who felt better being with her friends. Laura's routine went well until she missed a tumble and fell, about three-quarters of the way through. She got up and finished, but her heart wasn't in it. Carol and Todd felt crushed.

When the meet was over, Laura found her parents. She looked shaky and said that she was glad it was over. Todd and Carol were deeply disappointed by her performance, although they didn't say so; they had thought she had a chance to win a medal at this meet, and so had her coach. But Laura had been incapacitated by nerves, which is understandable in a nine-year-old. The family packed their stuff into the van as Linda told Laura how great she had done, which was her way of making everyone feel better but which seemed only to make Laura feel worse.

Laura didn't say a word the whole way home. Todd and Carol did their best to act as though nothing had happened, and Linda napped. When they stopped off for dinner at Laura's favorite restaurant, she finally started behaving a bit more like herself. But her confidence was shaken, and she was much quieter and more withdrawn than usual for the next several days. Her coach thought her confidence would return, but even she worried when Laura refused to do her balance-beam routine that Monday at practice.

As the days went by, Mrs. Pratt continued to press Laura about her reading. The class project was due, and Laura didn't have hers—she hadn't been able to finish the book. As the rest of the class presented their projects one by one over three days, Laura began feeling queasy again. The other kids seemed to have enjoyed reading their books and making dioramas, mobiles, costumes, and other props for their book presentations. One boy, Derrick, had even come in dressed as a pilgrim for his report on a book about early Colonial life. Laura knew she had let Mrs. Pratt down, and she didn't want to admit that she couldn't finish the book she'd been assigned. She felt wistful watching the other kids, who had done so much more than just read their books. Her classmates had really gotten into their projects, and Laura realized that she had missed out on something fun.

She walked up to Mrs. Pratt after lunch and said that she wanted another chance to try to make a report on her book. Mrs. Pratt was happy to give Laura another opportunity, but when she asked how Laura planned on finishing the book and completing the project, Laura didn't know what to say. "I would be glad to help you after school," Mrs. Pratt said. "Or maybe your mother or father could help—the other children's parents helped them with their reports. Do you think your parents would help?" Laura said that she would ask them, but she wondered when she would have the time to make a pilgrim costume or a diorama *after* finishing a whole book.

I would sooner read a timetable or a catalogue than nothing at all.
—W. SOMERSET MAUGHAM

THE PROBLEM

The situation with Laura and her family is fairly common: Kids today often lead busy, demanding lives, even when they're in elementary school. Organized athletics and team sports are a primary cause of kids' being scheduled up to their eyeballs. Music lessons, art lessons, and time with divorced parents who don't live with them also contribute to kids' tight schedules. Mirroring the trends in our society as a whole, kids are often expected to take on an enormous range of activities and responsibilities. But there is only so much a child can do and only so much organized activity a child can take, while still having time to be a kid and do what kids are supposed to be doing: learning and attending school, and playing and having fun as they grow up.

Parents' hearts are generally in the right place when they sign their children up for the countless activities that exist for kids today. Typically, they will tell you how if their child doesn't learn to swim or play the violin when young, she or he won't be able to learn as an adolescent and "catch up" later to all the kids who started at age six. What they say is true, if you accept their goal structure: When these parents talk about having their kids get the right start, they mean the right start so that the kids can perform or compete against other children and do well in organized events. These parents aren't talking about learning to play the flute for its own sake, or learning how to swim as recreation. It's a different mind-set, one in which kids' performance is viewed very seriously by parents and children alike.

For Todd and Carol, the problem was that their own lives minus their children were basically uneventful, boring, and going nowhere fast. Todd's job as a purchasing manager was stressful as hell but it wasn't exactly the stuff of which TV movies are made. Carol's job at the clothing store was equally if not more stressful, especially from September to January, but she got little juice from it; it was just a way to pay the bills and keep her kids in leotards. For some people, jobs like Todd's and Carol's become careers and lead to bigger and better jobs with more responsibilities. But neither Todd nor Carol was thrilled enough about what they did for a living to push for it to become more than a way to earn a check: Their priority was to spend more time with their children. They were passed over for promotions that demanded longer hours and travel, but they never resented it.

The parents made the children the center of their lives, and the children willingly cooperated, attending every lesson and event under the sun. The girls were getting exposure to many interesting aspects of life, and the importance of this exposure should not be ignored. But they were also suffering from the pressure of a too-busy schedule and too many parental demands, both time-wise and psychologically. Their parents were overly wrapped up in their performance at recitals and athletic events; they couldn't help it, the kids were their life. The kids felt this pressure and did their best to perform. But at eight or nine, there's only so much stress a child can take—and the amount she should be expected to take is considerably less even than this.

So what happened to Laura amid this sea of responsibilities? She was fine as long as school meant sitting at a desk in the classroom during regular school hours and doing what the teacher said. Laura was bright and took teacher direction extremely well, and she worked hard and applied herself to her tasks. This was fine for first and second grade. But now Laura was in third grade, and a new monkey wrench had been thrown into the gears. Emblazoned on its handle was the word *homework*. This was something new, and it sent Laura reeling. The realization hit her slowly that she wasn't reading as well as the other kids, that she didn't know the material, that she was falling behind in class discussions even though her attention rarely wandered. Why? Because the other children were doing *homework*, and they were doing it when they got home from school and were still fresh, not after dinner at 8:00 P.M. when they had gotten up at 6:15 A.M. and spent a day that would daunt Donald Trump.

Although Laura was now aware of the problem, it was easy to push it out of her mind because her mind's activities were accounted for virtually every waking moment of her day. Mrs. Pratt was more concerned than Laura by far—she saw that the priorities in Laura's home environment weren't on reading and academic performance, and she was worried that Laura would fall progressively further behind. Mrs. Pratt knew that Laura would need to depend on reading for many years after her last dismount from the parallel bars or half-gainer dive. But there wasn't much this teacher could do except to speak with Laura's mother (which she had already done) and continue to urge Laura to spend more time and effort on her homework. Mrs. Pratt already did everything she could to help Laura during the school day, but the school schedule was busy and there was little free time. What Laura needed was quiet time at home when she was well rested and fed, time she could spend reading, dreaming about projects, and crafting them, possibly with some help from Mom or Dad. Laura was artistically gifted, and there was no reason why she could not create one of the more impressive projects in the class—if only she had the time and energy.

Laura's problem with reading would soon be followed by problems with other academic classes. As the children began to be assigned more home reading, projects, and work in social studies, science, and math, Laura would fall further behind. Reading was the first clue that something was wrong—it was the first and most obvious casualty of her overcommitted schedule. But soon enough, as she proceeded through third grade and through the rest of elementary school, not having quality time to devote to homework would seriously and negatively impact Laura's academic progress.

The interrelationship of the homework problem and the problem with her parents meant that her folks didn't have the time or the inclination to actively help Laura with school assignments. Neither Todd nor Carol had loved school, although both had done reasonably well at it. They were not academically oriented people: When they thought about having fun with their children, they thought of going to activities and competitions, or going out to dinners or movies. Todd and Carol both felt that schoolwork should be able to be accomplished within the confines of the school day—that is, if Laura worked hard enough and didn't waste time like so many kids do. But this meant that Laura missed out on a very important part of being a kid: spending time learning about schoolwork with your parents by reading and talking about homework and projects. While other kids' parents were helping sew and dye pilgrim costumes, Laura's folks were driving her from one organized activity to another. While other kids' parents were helping make game boards for wood shop to demonstrate the games ancient Egyptians played, Carol and Todd were cheering at a diving meet. Yes, Todd and Carol spent time with their children—but the key here is that the time they spent was not used for joint work on projects and learning about school subjects.

Laura was missing out on the opportunity to share her school experience with her parents, to talk about projects and books and benefit from their mentorship. Psychologists talk often about the kind of dynamic that develops when a parent helps a child step by step through a project, working alongside the child, answering questions, guiding the project when the child falters, but allowing the child to do the bulk of the work. This parental behavior is called "scaffolding" because it does what a scaffold does: It helps a building "grow" strong and true. Todd and Carol gave their children lots of love and support, but they rarely provided any scaffolding in academic areas. Hence, the children didn't develop in these areas. Plus, the girls missed out on the one-on-one closeness and dynamic that develops when parents and children discover things and learn *together*.

Laura was trying through independent work completed in inadequate time to keep up with kids whose parents saw that they maintained a reasonable schedule and were available to answer questions and provide guidance. Laura could not possibly keep up, and she was sure to emerge the ultimate loser. Long after her awards, ribbons, and medals were locked in an old dusty trunk, Laura would be suffering from the lack of academic and thinking skills she could and should have developed when she was in elementary school. These skills can't be put on hold and worked on later, like a painting. The child grows up, and the opportunities to develop the skills pass by and close off. The child begins to perceive herself as slower or less smart than the others in her class—and the disasters that this lack of self-esteem can bring are many, and deeply destructive.

In fact, Laura showed the signs of performance anxiety already. Her nervousness and loss of appetite might have been normal for a child performing in a statewide competition, but isn't it worth asking whether competing was worth the stress it placed on Laura? Laura's participation in sports and other activities was a positive force in her life only as long as she enjoyed the time she spent on the activities and as long as they raised her self-esteem and feelings of self-efficacy. This is supposed to be the whole point of performing the activities. But when a child starts suffering from stress and falling asleep before dinner and never finishing the books she's assigned, parents should reexamine their motives for keeping the child in the activities. What was really going on in Laura's case? Of course it's obvious that her parents got their own juice from her and Linda, their superstar daughters. But whatever happened to just being a little kid? Adult life is long and filled with endless responsibilities. Laura and Linda deserved at least to be able to look back at one time in their early lives that was relatively carefree.

The sad fact is that Laura's awareness that she was beginning to lag behind the other children was making her act shy and more withdrawn. She didn't raise her hand in class as much as she used to, didn't volunteer answers because she worried that they were wrong. We can't afford to allow young children to lose their feelings of self-efficacy in school; the consequences can be disastrous. The athletics and music were supposed to enhance her self-image, but she felt so much pressure to earn a medal that when she didn't, she felt like a failure. Never mind the fact that her routine was better than those of a majority of kids her age on the team: Laura was focused on *winning* and scoring highly. Her father had convinced her that this was possible since he had done it. (Pressure, pressure, pressure.) Her mother had reminded her to set a good example for her sister. (Pressure.) When Laura slipped and fell during her routine, she felt inadequate. So instead of feeling smart in school and talented in athletics like she used to, now she felt like crying into her pillow. The kid lacked perspective on the situation—and it's not hard to understand why.

What's particularly sad about Laura's story is that she was bright and diligent, but she was still having trouble with her schoolwork. She worked hard at school, athletics, and everything else she did in life, but her commitments were getting away from her. She was like a gerbil on a big wheel spun by a motor, moving faster every day, until she was holding on instead of running. With the kind of raw material Laura had, she should have been supersuccessful at school. But she almost ended up on the recommended retention list to repeat the third grade. What went wrong?

I do not know any reading more easy, more fascinating, more delightful than a catalogue.
—ANATOLE FRANCE

LOSING STRATEGIES

Well-meaning people kept trying different strategies to help Laura. Unfortunately, more often than not they were *losing* strategies. They seemed logical at the time, and everyone truly wanted to help this nice little kid learn to read better and spend more time at it. So what did they do wrong?

The number-one losing strategy was Carol and Todd's decision to continue Laura's schedule of athletic activities despite the words of warning from Mrs. Pratt, as well as several of the couple's friends and other family members. Lots of people told Todd and Carol they were pushing their children too hard and too fast. But the parents didn't see it this way. They couldn't bear to scale back the sports because they saw gymnastics and diving as Laura's eventual ticket to college. She *was* a good gymnast, but so were thousands of other third graders across the country. And they couldn't stop the piano lessons, because Laura especially enjoyed them. As for the art lessons, they were Linda's favorite, and Laura would feel left out and denied if her sister took lessons without her. So, after discussing the situation, Todd and Carol agreed that Laura's reading problem would have to be solved, but that the solution would not include her dropping important activities that could lead to opportunities in the future.

Coming in a close second as the biggest losing strategy was Carol's insistence that Laura spend one hour (or even more) on reading every night after dinner, without regard for what Laura's day had been like. This is a good example of why you can't just take strategies out of a book without thinking about how they affect *your* kid. In many cases, having a child read for an hour after dinner might be a good idea. But in Laura's case, she hit the floor running just after 6:00 A.M. and didn't stop until dinner was cleaned up at 7:30 P.M. Her day usually included at least one athletic workout, sometimes two, and on those days when she worked out only once, a music or art lesson. Then the girls helped their mother or father prepare and serve dinner and helped clean up afterward.

These were little kids, not Arnold Schwarzenegger and Hulk Hogan: They needed rest, and by 7:30 or 8:00 P.M., they were ready to relax for an hour and go to bed. Insisting that a child who is having reading problems read every night when she is absolutely exhausted is not a good way to prove to the child that she *can* read. If Laura sits down with a tough book when her eyes are closing and her brain is fuzzy, she'll end her day on a negative note, feeling like an ineffectual loser. What Laura needs is regimented reading time, but when both her energy level and commitment to the task are high.

The parents' third brilliant idea had to do with Laura's weekend free time, which was not voluminous to start with. Todd and Carol thought it would be a good idea for Laura to spend her spare time on weekends reading in an undisturbed environment. So they started rushing her home from practices and meets and classes and recitals, feeding her a quick lunch or dinner, and sending her to her room alone. Meanwhile the parents and Linda would watch a video or television, run an errand, or whatever. Maybe if the others had used this time to clean the oven or toilets, Laura would have felt that parity was achieved. But as it was, she felt like an inmate sentenced to more time while the wardens and another inmate kicked off their shoes and ordered a pizza. Laura saw reading as her punishment, as something she was sent alone to her room to do. Her sister didn't have to be alone—*she* got to watch great movies and bake cookies and make popcorn with their father. So instead of working earnestly on her reading, Laura would get angry and start feeling sorry for herself for being locked up with a stupid book on Saturday afternoon or evening when the rest of the family had a good time. Care to place a bet on how much actual *reading* she did on these occasions?

The mistake the parents were making was even bigger than it first appeared. Not only were they sending Laura to her room on weekends to work on reading while the rest of the family bonded and relaxed, but, significantly, they were sending her there *alone*. Todd and Carol weren't helping Laura with her reading. They acted as if sending her off to read alone was taking care of the problem. The fact was that Laura's parents didn't enjoy academics and reading much themselves, so they didn't relish the idea of sitting with Laura going over boring books. That was Mrs. Pratt's job! Laura was a smart girl, and she got the message: Her parents didn't enjoy reading, they didn't want to help her with reading, and reading wasn't worth their time. The bottom line was that reading was viewed by Laura as a punishment, not something fun. Reading also became something that distanced Laura from her family, a negative influence in her young life.

Todd and Carol thought Laura needed independent work on reading, independent practice rehearsing what she was learning in school. But Laura was too young, too inexperienced as a reader, and too insecure in her ability to spend long hours poring over books alone. This is another reason the "go read alone" strategy was a loser with Laura. Laura was excellent at taking direction from others. She spent her entire day taking direction from her mother, her coach, Mrs. Pratt, her art teacher, her music teacher, her father, you name it. Laura's life consisted of being told exactly what to do and how to do it, and then taking the time to apply herself to the task: She was a diligent, hardworking child. But one thing she was not at this point in her life was a particularly creative or independent child. Laura was also highly dependent on receiving approval from her parents, teachers, and coach: she needed this approval regularly to feel good about herself. By structuring Laura's life as they had, her parents had created or at least encouraged these personality characteristics in their daughter. They had, in effect, taught their daughter to become a person who took direction well and worked hard to apply herself within the limits of instruction. They *hadn't* taught Laura to be a self-starter who figured things out on her own. She never had the time or opportunity to learn to think independently. Every moment of her day was scheduled by others.

What did all this mean when it came to Laura's reading problem? For one thing, it meant that Laura desperately needed someone to sit with her and show her the way through her books, to sit with her and encourage her to try, and to praise her when she succeeded. Laura needed approval from her parents when she read well, but they were nowhere in sight. By abandoning Laura when she needed support, Todd and Carol created negative feelings and anxiety, all of which became bound up with reading in Laura's mind. From her point of view, there were few if any rewards for the time she spent reading alone at home. Under these circumstances, she would have far rather burned her books than read them.

When Laura was in a gymnastics or diving meet or a piano recital, her parents talked about it incessantly and drove through four-foot snow drifts to attend. These events were family affairs. Her parents also liked talking with Laura about the intricacies of her performances, and they provided her with feedback and positive reinforcement for her successes. These events were what this family enjoyed. But when Laura had to prepare a book report and project for Mrs. Pratt, her parents were obviously bored by the discussions Laura attempted to start. Should she paint a special set of illustrations for the book? Should she write a poem or song about the main characters? These were Mrs. Pratt's suggestions, but Laura wasn't sure which suggestion was best. She needed her parents to get excited about the task, help her choose a focus and get started, and sit with her as she planned the steps needed to get the project done.

Instead, Laura found her parents didn't want to get so involved with her reading projects. They were willing to make the time for her to read alone in her room. In their eyes, this was their role—the way they saw it, they were reorganizing the family's time around Laura's needs. They wanted to be spending their time with both of their children doing the types of activities the family enjoyed. Instead, they were home watching videos because of Laura's reading problem. You can see why this situation was like a volcano waiting to erupt. Both parties—Laura on the one hand and her parents on the other—felt like they were doing their best and felt put upon by the demands of the situation. Laura got no direct help with reading, and her parents obviously weren't interested when she talked about her ideas for book reports. The messages Laura got were loud and clear, and she became even more turned off to reading.

Another losing strategy was Laura's parents' decision not to worry about recommendations made by Mrs. Pratt and others concerning the negative influence of Laura's peer group on her attitude toward reading. Mrs. Pratt had pointed out that an unfortunate side effect of Laura's heavy involvement in athletics and artistic activities was that she was surrounded by other kids who also made these events central in their lives. Obviously, if the kids were attending these extracurricular activities, they weren't at after-school library hours, and they weren't home doing projects on books. Mrs. Pratt and other teachers had noted that Laura could use some positive role models to encourage her to read and see the enjoyment reading can bring. But Laura's friends were mostly other gymnasts and divers. She didn't have as much time as most kids to spend with friends anyway, and one thing Laura had never experienced was time spent with friends who loved reading and shared this activity with Laura.

For example, had Laura attended a library reading hour, she would have gotten to know classmates and other kids who enjoyed books, who got excited about reading, and who spent a lot of time on school projects. This peer group would have influenced Laura positively in a direction in which she desperately needed a positive influence. As it was, Laura never spent any time with other children who loved books. It wasn't surprising that she didn't see how wonderful reading could be.

All of the losing strategies her parents tried grew from an earnest desire on their part to help Laura. Carol and Todd just couldn't see what they were doing wrong. Laura needed winning strategies to turn her sit-

uation around while there was still time to set her on
the reading track.

*Nothing links man to man like the frequent passage from hand
to hand of a good book.*
—WALTER SICKERT

WINNING STRATEGIES

The biggest overall winning strategy for Laura has to
do with a redefinition of the family's goals for their children. Like many problems with reading, Laura's problem was more far-reaching than it might have seemed at
first. Laura's parents are at the root of the problem, and
the solution must begin with them. Carol and Todd
must develop a more balanced view of what life for a
nine-year-old should be. They should ask themselves
about what Laura will remember when she looks back
on her childhood: Are all of her activities really necessary? Laura needs more time for herself, more time for
play and quiet thinking and reflection, more time during which books can play a central role. There must be
a redefinition of the family's attitudes towards childhood and what's important for children to do with their
time.

Laura and her family were actually very fortunate:
Laura was young and only just beginning to display a
problem with reading. She had a dedicated teacher
who wanted to head off the problem before it became
an overarching problem with school and academics in
general. Laura was a hardworking child who would benefit greatly from help with her reading: She knew how
to apply herself and possessed self-control and disci-

pline unusual in a nine-year-old. All she needed was the right structure around her, the right scaffold to build the foundation of solid reading skills.

Many children fail to read as much as they should because they are awed and numbed by video games and other cheap thrills that take far less effort than sitting down with a good book. These kids are used to life coming easy: They get by in school with minimal effort, then they go home to be passively entertained by the products of the computer age. Kids like these are more common than kids like Laura, and the parents of kids like these are often more aware of their children's problem with reading than are parents of kids like Laura. It's important to remember, though, that superbusy, productive, and successful children like Laura may need help with reading too.

Laura wasn't spending her afternoons and evenings like a zombie in front of the computer or television screen. That wasn't her style. In fact, Laura competently handled the near-adult-level responsibilities and stresses that came with her athletic and other involvements. This child knew that life didn't drop success in her lap: She knew she had to work hard for her goals. But Laura was missing out on some essential aspects of being a kid. The main task her parents and teachers faced was to provide Laura a more balanced life in which she could develop and grow to her potential. The issue was what this balance would mean in terms of Laura's daily activities—and what it would mean to Todd and Carol, who were so wrapped up in their children's accomplishments.

So, winning strategy number one is for Todd, Carol, and Laura to sit down as a family and discuss a relaxing of the current frantic schedule. Some activities Laura currently engages in will have to be suspended for a while. This doesn't mean Laura will never take art class again, for example; it just means she will rotate through several activities over time rather than cram all of them into the same week. The family should decide which activities are best for Laura, not for her parents. It seems as though Laura has been experiencing quite a bit of stress lately as a result of athletic competitions: Maybe she should take time off from organized athletics for a while. Or maybe she should drop piano and art classes. The decision should be a joint one, but the main emphasis should be on what Laura really wants. It could be that having a father who won so many medals for swimming was placing too much stress on Laura. Maybe she would have preferred to take art and piano classes and spend her other time with her friends just playing and being a kid. Which specific activities she drops is not the issue: What matters is that her schedule be relaxed to make time for academics. And of course the problems Laura is having will be re-created in a year or two with Linda, so coming up with a solution now is doubly imperative.

Winning strategy number two is for Laura's parents to change their goals for her life. Right now they want her to do well in school, it's true, but most important, they want her to win at athletics and perform well at recitals. What gets Carol and Todd excited now is when both of their daughters win medals in diving or gymnastics or place well in a piano competition. This is a lot of emphasis on *competing* and *winning*. Carol and Todd are driving the message home that life means competing and winning, and that with enough hard work their children can, indeed, win. All of this emphasis on the ultimate outcomes of performance is disadvantageous and disabling to Laura and Linda. It is good to teach children that hard work is necessary to success. But it is better to stress the value of effort itself and personal improvement as their own rewards, rather than focus on the outcome of beating others and excelling.

Each child will have her or his own areas of expertise in life, areas in which she or he can win and be better than others. But it's far more typical in life *not* to win: We aren't always best at everything we do, and it's better for kids to learn this lesson early. Just because a child can't win at something by being the best at it does not mean she shouldn't try. For instance, perhaps Laura wouldn't become the best reader in her class, but with effort she could become a competent reader. She was a disciplined child who was willing to put in effort— but only if it meant she could win. As it became obvious to Laura that she wasn't gifted in reading and that other children were better at it, her desire and motivation to push forward with reading waned. *Why bother,* she reasoned, *if I can't be one of the best?* This attitude was a natural extension of Laura's tutelage at the hands of her father, who believed that winning was everything. Although she was capable of becoming a solid reader, she didn't see the point if it meant being second best.

Another problem with the focus on performance on the part of Laura's family was that it emphasized the extrinsic rewards of success rather than the intrinsic rewards of effort. Laura was taught by her parents to value the medals and awards that were the tangible evidence of success. There was tension before all competitions and recitals and a general perception that the goal was to win. When Laura slipped up, her parents became noticeably depressed, although they tried not to show it. Positive performance at practice sessions was discussed as a sure sign that Laura was capable of winning—not as an end in itself. In other words, Laura could have learned that the time and effort she put into athletics and piano was valuable in itself, even if she didn't excel.

The way to teach Laura this intrinsic pleasure in learning and practicing would have been to reward it by placing less emphasis on competition and on proving herself publicly. Had her parents focused instead on the joy of athletics and music, Laura would have learned to share that joy and concentrate on the experience rather than to obsess on the outcome. Did it really matter that her dismount from the parallel bars wasn't flawless, and that this would mean she would sacrifice the medal at the next competition? Wasn't it more important for Laura to love gymnastics, feel good about herself as she practiced, and see herself improving? It's clear that Laura's mind-set prepared her for working hard and placing pressure on herself to succeed. But it didn't prepare her for loving what she was doing regardless of whether she won or lost.

What does all this have to do with Laura's reading? A lot. Laura needs to learn to experience the joy of reading and see it as an end in itself rather than simply a way to achieve a grade. Children who focus on the outcomes of successful reading—an *A* in English and better grades in general—will not continue to read for fun as they grow up. Once the grades have been earned, these kids will lose interest in reading. The goal is to turn kids on to the *joy* of reading, and Laura's parents were doing just about everything wrong.

This brings us to a third, very influential winning strategy. For Laura to show a real and immediate improvement in reading, she needs an environment that's designed for reading. Here again it's up to Todd and

Carol. Up until now, their lives have been antibook: They watch a lot of television and read a rag of a newspaper, and reading doesn't have much of a place in their lives. This will have to change if the children are going to grow up to read well and often. Carol should make a spot in the home where books are kept and displayed, a place where the girls can reach out and pick up a book. Books should be left out where the girls spend their time, too—on the coffee table, next to the dining table, and on the girls' dressers. The key is that books must be made *easily available*.

The next key is that the books must be interesting and relevant to the girls' lives. Given how broad the children's interests are, there are many excellent book options for this family. Bookstores and libraries are filled with volumes about gymnastics, diving, athletics in general, piano, drawing and painting, you name it. There are how-to books in each of these areas, plus novels about kids who participate in these activities. There are also wonderful stories for young girls and boys about children their own age and the problems they face adjusting to school, getting along with others, coping with their parents' divorce, keeping up with their schoolwork, and so on. By choosing some appropriate titles and leaving them where the girls will see them, Carol can ensure that the girls will be better exposed to books. A weekly trip to the library after school would also be a terrific idea—it could replace one other activity the girls have been involved in. Carol could take both girls to the library reading hour, then spend another hour looking for books, talking to librarians for advice, and generally getting the kids used to being around books.

Of course, there are many ways to get Laura turned on to reading: There are magazines related to her athletic interests (a subscription would make a good birthday or holiday present); there are young-adult novels for nine-year-olds; there are comic books and other humorous materials. Reading can be fun, and Laura will be more likely to learn that fact if she is given some fun reading material! Carol could help Laura overcome her trepidation by reading aloud to the children: For example, she might begin a simple book likely to be interesting to the girls, then stop to prepare dinner . . . and leave the book out on the table. Laura would be likely to pick up the book sooner or later.

Other techniques to help create a positive reading environment in the home include asking Laura to pick movies for the family to see based on her perusal of movie reviews, having the children work together to create a family game (like Trivial Pursuit with questions about athletics or some other topic the girls like), and having Laura read and collect recipes that she and her mother could cook together. Laura could create a family scrapbook containing pictures and descriptions of vacations, trips, swim meets, gymnastics competitions, piano recitals, or whatever she wants. She could also draft a family telephone and address book—anything, as long as it involves reading and using the written word. Laura could clip and read coupons, and if she helps with the marketing she could be allowed to keep the money that's saved and apply it toward the purchase of a book.

These are just examples—there are more ideas in the list at the end of this book. What these recommendations share is that they place reading front and center amid the flurry of the family's daily life. If Laura comes to see the value of information gathered through reading, she will begin to see reading as a worthwhile and pleasurable activity for reasons that go way beyond getting good grades. And Laura's father should get in on the act too—he isn't much of a book lover, but he could make an effort to change for the good of his children (and himself!). Laura needs to see both her parents—the most influential people in her life—reading and enjoying it. She doesn't need to be harangued about her reading level and falling grades, and she doesn't need to be sent to her room alone to read. There has to be a paradigm shift toward an atmosphere in which reading is fun, valuable, and a part of everyday life.

Mrs. Pratt, who is certainly willing to help Laura, has many good ideas. If Laura's parents start bringing Laura to the after-school library reading hours, Mrs. Pratt will be pleased and will start making other suggestions. Laura could be given special reading material for class projects if that would help get her started. (Maybe Laura isn't interested in the books Mrs. Pratt usually assigns!) Mrs. Pratt could be consulted by Carol and Todd and used as a resource, and during school hours Mrs. Pratt could make an extra effort to reinforce every minute Laura spends reading. She could also avoid asking Laura to read aloud before the whole class, because this could cause embarrassment until Laura comes up to her classmates' level. Instead, Laura could practice reading aloud in a group of students who are having similar problems.

There are many options for helping Laura, but they all depend on her having the time to sit down with a book and really focus on and think about it. This is the biggest change that's needed, and once the time is made available, the winning strategies described here can combine to carry Laura forward with her reading. Once Laura is enabled through changes in her environment to experience the joy of reading, her natural self-discipline and hardworking nature will take over and she will become one of those children who can't put books down.

Just the knowledge that a good book is awaiting one at the end of a long day makes that day happier.
—KATHLEEN NORRIS

MORALS OF LAURA'S STORY

How to Get and Keep Kids Reading

• *You* must make reading a priority if you expect your child to do so. Ask yourself how much emphasis you've placed on reading in the past. If the answer is "not much," this could explain your child's problem.

• If your child participates in many after-school activities, limit these activities to make more time for reading, daydreaming, and just being a kid. Kids won't learn to enjoy reading without adequate opportunities.

• If you can't remember the last three books your child was assigned, you should get more involved in what your child is reading for school.

• Consider your child's style. Some children are self-starters who will pick up books on their own; others expect and need guidance and direction from parents and teachers to get them going.

• If you often emphasize winning and excelling to your child, you may be teaching her that being the number-one reader in the class is all that matters. Emphasize instead that *working* on reading is what's important, not being the best.

• Don't send off one child to read alone while you enjoy yourself with a sibling. You'll give the impression that you don't care about helping the reluctant reader, that you prefer the other child, and that you're just trying to get rid of the reluctant reader and her problem.

• If your child introduces the topic of reading—for a school project, for homework, or for a report—immediately engage yourself in conversation. Act interested and provide your child with information and support to complete the tasks.

• If you are highly involved in your child's after-school activities and find yourself spending all your free time encouraging these activities, you may be discouraging your child's *academic* growth. Aim for more of a balance in your own and your child's life.

• If you never read and rarely use information from books, you are setting a bad example for your child. Let your child see you reading often and enjoying using what you've read.

• If your child's teachers, other parents, and your friends keep giving you the same advice about your child, it may be worth listening to—these people could have valuable insights into the reading problem.

CHAPTER FOUR

THE VIDEO GAME MONSTER: JEREMY'S STORY

*A good book should leave you . . . slightly exhausted at the end.
You live several lives while reading it.*
—WILLIAM STYRON

Jeremy walked home from school the long way again to avoid seeing anyone he knew. "I hate my braces, I hate my zits, I look like such a nerd," he kept muttering. It had been months since Jeremy could look in the mirror without grimacing. Twelve was a tough age. Most of the other sixth-grade boys were taller and older-looking than he, and he didn't appreciate the fact that all the girls resembled Amazon women. Just yesterday Jeremy had offered to walk Sharene home. He had been cultivating a big crush on her for weeks, and he had finally gotten up the nerve to take her hand . . . which, to his horror, he discovered was about three sizes larger than his! Then there was the humiliation he'd endured when he decided to give Sharene a kiss on the cheek. He had to find a curb edging the walkway that he could balance on just so he'd be tall enough. *I'll never make it to my teenage years,* Jeremy thought. *I'll die of embarrassment first!*

Jeremy was in sixth grade, his first year of middle school, in a suburb of a big California city. His father and he had just moved to California from New Jersey, where Jeremy had grown up. Last year Jeremy's mother had died of cancer, and it was just his father, Earl, and Jeremy now. His father had picked California as their way of starting over. Plus, he had gotten a good job with a local affiliate of the courier company where he'd worked as a manager. Now, Earl and Jeremy were house hunting. It had been a tough year for both of them, but things were finally starting to look up.

Jeremy liked his new school well enough, but he had never been really school-oriented. His mom used to sit with him and help with his homework every night. "Just one more page and I'll get you a slice of pie," she used to say. Jeremy had never been a terrific student, but he had never failed, either. It's just that school didn't float his boat. What got Jeremy excited were the typical Y-chromosome activities his father had passed down— cars, race cars, dreams of his own someday-car, and sports. He also enjoyed building things out of wood or spare parts from all the appliances he had disassembled. The key was that Jeremy loved doing things that involved working with his hands: The kid had the manual dexterity of a spider monkey. He could learn from watching his dad or a mechanic or even a show on TV, then he'd take things apart and put them back together and make them work again. But most of all, like many other boys his age, Jeremy loved video games. Whether played at an arcade—where Jeremy hemorrhaged money to maintain his habit—or at home on his 29-inch mega-TV, video games were the panacea for Jeremy's problems, the cure for his loneliness, the imaginary world he retreated to whenever the real world didn't measure up.

Jeremy didn't have many friends in his new neighborhood yet, but he had made a few, especially Sharene. Today he got home, poured a glass of milk, took a whole package of chocolate chip cookies off the shelf, and headed to his room. His mom would have killed him if she had been around. But now that it was just Jeremy and Earl, the standards had gotten a bit lax. He wondered if all that stuff about chocolate and pimples was true, as he ate his seventh Monster Chipper. Jeremy sat back, turned on the TV, and got out his latest, greatest video game (at least that's what the box said: The game had something to do with simian aliens who bite off earth-dwellers' and smaller simians' heads for 250 bananas apiece). Unwilling to hog the entire experience to himself, he picked up the phone and called his friend Dan, inviting him over to participate in the cannibalization ritual. Ten minutes later Dan was at the door. Five minutes after that the boys sat munching cookies and battling an invading baboon army with the seriousness of Stormin' Norman Schwarzkopf, their reality fading into stylized simian heaven.

When Earl got home from work he wasn't pleased. It was clear that the boys had spent three hours eating cookies and beating each other's brains out (and eating them) in a virtual world with Jeremy's new video game. (The game did look intriguing, Earl had to admit.) Earl had already spoken to Jeremy twice this week about his homework, but nothing he did seemed to make any difference. This moment wasn't the time, though, because Earl was tired and needed some dinner, and there was nobody to make it except him. So he grabbed a box of pasta and a jar of sauce and yelled in to the bedroom to see if Dan would be joining them for the meal. Dan agreed, eager to participate in the conversation about sports, cars and simian invaders instead of heading home to hear his mother and two sisters talk about their interests, which he found far less compelling.

As the boys sat down, Earl dished up the pasta into huge mounds and covered them with sauce and cheese. Just what the three wanted—nothing fancy, and plenty of it. Talk drifted to cars, of course, then baseball, then hockey, then professional sports teams in general. Faces became red with tomato sauce as the boys argued about the advantages of east- versus west-coast teams. Talk of professional sports then became talk of the boys' own favorite sport: the unofficial simian-invader Olympics that Jeremy was hosting every day after school. Earl was enjoying the conversation, but he was too beat to compete for air time. So he picked up the plates and asked the kids what they wanted for dessert. Afraid that his father would learn the horrible truth about the Monster Chippers, Jeremy said (maybe a bit too quickly), "Oh, nothing, Dad . . . we're stuffed!" and then he and Dan got up from the table and ran back to his room.

Earl finished doing the dishes and turned on the television in the living room. His body felt like lead. It was tough getting by without his wife, Jean; she'd done so much for him and Jeremy. Jean would have been going over Jeremy's homework and helping him with his reading right now and giving him practice tests to get his grades up, Earl thought, but he was just too tired; plus he didn't know that stuff. He'd never been much of a student and had forgotten most of what he'd learned in school. Earl knew he wasn't up to the task of helping Jeremy. The boy would just have to do it on his own, the way Earl always had—and he'd gotten through school okay . . . not great, but at least he'd graduated. Some medical drama advertised as "riveting" droned in the background as Earl's mind drifted. He had almost fallen asleep when the sound of the boys' laughter jarred him, mixed with the electronic shrieks of cannibalized simians. Earl knew that his son should be doing his schoolwork, but Jeremy sounded so happy in there—the boys were just being boys and having a great time. *I wish we had games like that when I was a kid,* Earl thought. He couldn't bring himself to break it up, so instead he fell asleep on the couch with his feet on the coffee table, shoes still on.

The next day at school Jeremy sank down in his seat like a lizard—this was one time when being small for his age helped! He didn't want his social studies teacher to call on him because he hadn't read the book chapter about the pioneer West. It looked so boring and miserable to Jeremy, and he'd had far better things to do. Now he sat doodling Corvettes and monolithic killer baboons in the margin of his pristine notebook. Sharene sat across the room, her head high above the sea of short boys. Jeremy wrote "Sharene" in his notebook next to his own name. The moment of tranquillity was abruptly halted:

"Jeremy! Please pay attention, dear. I know you're new here, but it would help to listen in class. What do you think it would have been like to be a pioneer in the old West? Would you have enjoyed living back then, a hundred fifty years ago?"

Mrs. Smyth sat on her desk. She was a fantastic teacher, and all the kids liked her. She did her best to bring the material to life. Her hair was falling loose from her bun, she was perennially disorganized, but she had a pleasant face and a warm smile and plenty of time to help. Jeremy liked Mrs. Smyth, too—but that couldn't substitute for having read the book.

"Well, Mrs. Smyth, I don't know . . ." Jeremy said. "I guess it would have been awful to live before there were video games!" The class snorted and laughed.

"Do you think not having *video games* was the worst thing the pioneers faced?" asked Mrs. Smyth.

"Uhhhh, no . . . they didn't have cars or plumbing or heating either!" The class laughed again, and Mrs. Smyth joined them this time.

"Yes, all of that is true, Jeremy. But can you tell me about some of the problems they did face?"

Jeremy looked around nervously. "Not really," he said in a whisper.

"Why don't we talk a bit more about it after class?" Mrs. Smyth said gently, moving on to another child.

Jeremy felt dejected. He was so far behind with his schoolwork that there didn't seem any point in trying to catch up anymore. Mrs. Smyth was a lot nicer to him than the other teachers—they snapped at him and told him to work harder, which didn't help much. But Mrs. Smyth was a kind person, and she knew that Jeremy had lost his mother last year. Twelve is a tough age for any kid, and Jeremy was dealing with a new school, a new home in a new part of the country, and a redefined relationship with his father—all without the help of his mother, who had always been close to Jeremy. So Mrs. Smyth went easy, trying to pry Jeremy loose from the shell he entered every time he walked through the doors of the school building.

"Hey, Jeremy, how's it going?" she asked. Jeremy looked down and studied the neon-orange laces on his high-tops. "Don't worry, Jeremy. I'll help you with your reading. Now, why don't you tell me what you usually do when you get home from school. How do you spend your time every afternoon?" Mrs. Smyth questioned Jeremy, trying her best to get an idea of how she could help, what she could say to Jeremy's father, what the school could do—anything. Jeremy talked slowly, hardly the same child who had described the hostile simian conquest in lurid detail to his father at the dinner table the night before. He acted like it was an inquisition. But Mrs. Smyth got enough details to figure out that Jeremy spent absolutely no time on his schoolwork and reading at home. It was no wonder he's falling so far behind.

Later that afternoon, Mrs. Smyth called Jeremy's father. She explained how much she liked Jeremy and that she recognized that the family had experienced a very sad year. She also said that Jeremy wasn't doing any homework and was falling behind, and that he didn't pay attention in class. "As Jeremy gets more and more out of touch with what the other children are reading and learning, he follows less and less of the classroom discussion," she explained.

Earl listened with concern. "But what should I do about it?" he asked. "My wife used to take care of all the reading and school stuff with Jeremy. I'm beat at the end of the day, and Jeremy's hungry, and the laundry needs doing, and the place needs straightening up, and the bills need to be paid. I just don't have the time!"

Mrs. Smyth made several suggestions, then added, "Even if you only read and worked with Jeremy for thirty or forty-five minutes a night it would make an enormous difference. He needs support in the home, from you, to learn to place the appropriate value upon school."

"I was never great in school myself," Earl replied.

"That doesn't matter to Jeremy," said Mrs. Smyth. "What Jeremy needs is for you to work with him and talk about what he's doing in school."

Earl hung up the phone and exhaled long and deep. He knew that Mrs. Smyth was right, but he also knew that he wasn't the right one to help Jeremy: He just didn't know how. He hated all the stuff about history, and all he remembered about book reports was how boring the books were. He didn't blame Jeremy for tuning out, although he would never say that to his son. *He's sure my kid,* Earl chucked to himself. *He loves to do things with his hands, but he doesn't see why he should spend all that time buried in books.* Earl decided that he should get home earlier to help Jeremy—but just as he was thinking about what specifically he could do to help, there was an emergency with a plane in Chicago that was carrying a major cargo shipment, and Earl ended up staying at the office until seven o'clock that evening.

Later that week, during lunch break, Sharene asked Jeremy if he wanted to try out for the school play. She was excited because the play was *Guys and Dolls* and she thought she was a natural to play the female lead. She even knew the songs because her parents always played the soundtracks of Broadway shows at home. "Come on, Jeremy—you'd be perfect! It's a play about real men who gamble and go to horse races, and you're from New Jersey! You'd fit the bill perfectly. You've got to come to tryouts next week!" Sharene was so psyched up that she could barely contain herself—she was giggling and bumping into Jeremy every time she started a sentence. But Jeremy looked glum. "What's the matter?" she asked.

Jeremy looked down and swallowed. "I could never be in a play," he said. "I wouldn't be able to memorize my lines. I'd forget my part. I'd mess up and look like an idiot and embarrass everyone, including you! How about if I just go to the play instead?"

"Oh, Jeremy," Sharene said, "you're so silly! You'd be great . . . just promise to think about it, okay?" Jeremy nodded his head, but he knew they'd be more likely to find an honest cardsharp than to see him in *Guys and Dolls*.

As Jeremy and Sharene walked back into the school building they saw Mrs. Smyth talking to the school principal, Mrs. Franklin. "It's such a shame about Jeremy," Mrs. Smyth was saying. "He's a sweet child, but he acts like he's been hit by a truck. He just doesn't care about school, and there's no one to help him. I'm doing my best to keep him involved so he doesn't end up tuning out completely."

Mrs. Franklin looked concerned. "The poor kid. He's been through so much. It's a tough age to lose your mother." Mrs. Smyth nodded in agreement. "Can't his father help?" asked Mrs. Franklin.

"I've tried calling a couple of times," said Mrs. Smyth, "but I guess he must be really busy or else he just doesn't want to get involved with Jeremy's reading problem and schoolwork."

"Well, someone's got to reach out to the boy," said Mrs. Franklin, as she and Mrs. Smyth watched Jeremy and Sharene walk down the hall to class, hand in hand.

* * *

Language is the soul of intellect, and reading is the essential process by which that intellect is cultivated beyond the commonplace experiences of everyday life.
—CHARLES SCRIBNER

THE PROBLEM

There was much more than the obvious problem going on with Jeremy. Yes, losing his mother was a significant tragedy at age twelve, but many children have had to face the loss of a parent, whether through death or divorce. Households break up and family dynamics change and need to be redefined. Jeremy was fortunate to have had a wonderful mother who spent a lot of time working with him at home, helping him with his reading and schoolwork. He wasn't the brightest kid in the world in the strictly academic sense—he didn't like abstract problems on paper that didn't mean anything to him, and he didn't like reading dumb textbooks and working on sentence fill-ins and other seemingly meaningless exercises. But Jeremy's mother had known that he was gifted in other ways, and she had used his interests and special talents to draw him into his schoolwork. Without her influence, though, Jeremy was floundering, and if nothing changed, a few years down the road he was likely to become a school dropout or at least a phase-out.

Jeremy's mom had helped maintain his self-esteem, but these days Jeremy didn't feel too great about himself. Like many kids his age, he looked gawky and poorly proportioned and had facial breakouts. He had just moved across the country, leaving behind his home and his friends and the security of the school he had attended since kindergarten. His mother wasn't there to help, and his father was working too hard to make a living for both of them to be of much help to Jeremy with his personal issues. Lost amid this backdrop of problems, Jeremy had floundered, focusing at first on the things in life he knew he could do well: building model cars and generally doing projects that involved working with his hands. He had an unusual talent for these types of activities, and he also had a terrific sense of design and proportion—his woodshop projects were always the best in the class, and he was one kid whose father didn't dread getting something homemade for Father's Day.

Lately, however, Jeremy's active interest in model cars and other projects had gradually been supplanted by a slide into the passive world of the video junkie. Like other activities that require hand-eye coordination, video games drew on the quick reflexes and skillful coordination that were Jeremy's hallmark, and he was progressively losing more and more of himself to the virtual reality of video games. The sad thing about Jeremy's (or any kid's) addiction to video games is that these games represent an unproductive, uncreative, often violent, and passive (but nevertheless mesmerizing) waste of time. Jeremy wasn't learning or growing—and he certainly wasn't reading or developing a love for books; he was killing time and brain cells in front of a television or arcade-game screen.

Considering how Jeremy spent his time, his problems at school were certainly understandable. But these problems were not going to go away by themselves, and no one was making any headway in dealing with them. Jeremy read only at the third-grade level; he could no longer keep up with the other children in class when they discussed reading assignments and passages from books. His performance in math and science wasn't as bad as in English and social studies, but at best he was doing only average work. Where Jeremy shone, predictably, was in shop classes that involved independent project design and work. But reading and performing well in all areas of school were well within his grasp, if only he would apply himself.

Despite Earl's caring deeply for his son, he had allowed the home atmosphere to become completely nonacademic—there was no expectation that Jeremy's reading and homework would be completed every night and no discussion about exactly what Jeremy's assignments were. There also was no limit placed on Jeremy's time in front of the TV mauling simian intruders. Earl barely had the energy to keep the house together and perform well at his new job. Earl always felt behind, and as he struggled to keep up with the housecleaning, the cooking, the shopping, the laundry, the bills, and everything else that running a household entails, he forgot to place Jeremy's school needs on a par with his other responsibilities.

There was another side to Earl's contribution to the problem, as well: He was embarrassed by his own poor performance in school, so he didn't want to sit down to work with Jeremy and end up displaying his ignorance like a peacock's tail. Earl had negative memories of school, and he had never liked people who talked about how well they did in school, what school they went to, how great learning was—you know the type. Actually, Earl had never trusted these sorts of people, and he was unconsciously passing on these biases and prejudices to his son. The trouble was that Jeremy would be held back by Earl's beliefs, since Jeremy could not help but identify with his father's values. And this was unfair to Jeremy: Just because his father had gotten only so far in life doesn't mean Jeremy should have to pick up the same burden and carry it another generation. But Earl didn't see it this way; from his point of view, he was doing what he thought was best for his son.

Then of course there was Mrs. Smyth, who so clearly could have been part of the solution had Jeremy's father agreed to implement some of her suggestions. Mrs. Smyth wanted Jeremy to join the after-school reading group she led. But Jeremy didn't want to (for obvious reasons), and Earl didn't see much point in forcing him when he'd rather be home playing video games and working on his classic-model-car collection. Mrs. Smyth also thought that the upcoming school play would be a great way for Jeremy to meet more kids, make friends, and start feeling more at home in the school environment. But Jeremy was terrified that his reading problem would hinder and embarrass him in front of the others—plus, he thought he looked like a nerd. Earl thought the play sounded like fun, but again, he didn't know how to encourage Jeremy without forcing him, which didn't strike Earl as a good idea.

The situation for Jeremy was bleak. Research shows that the middle-school years are a critical time when students either remain engaged in school or begin the process of dropping out as they enter and proceed through adolescence. Jeremy's lack of interest in school wasn't going to cure itself. And his poor reading ability would hurt him countless times and in countless ways in the future. Jeremy's other abilities were impressive—but it was tough to imagine how he would be able to capitalize on his talents and strengths without reasonable school and reading skills. Given his talents, it's clear that his ultimate career choices would probably involve using his design and mechanical abilities, but not many doors are open to people who can't read well. Plus, Jeremy's negative attitude toward school and learning essentially meant that he wouldn't be able to move forward in any area of knowledge or expertise: Instead of learning through reading and studying on his own, listening in class, and making full use of the educational experience, he would know only what he had been directly taught by others in those few courses in which he paid attention. What had Jeremy's father and the school tried to do to turn Jeremy's situation around?

What is reading but silent conversation?
—WALTER SAVAGE LANDOR

LOSING STRATEGIES

Unfortunately for Jeremy, a lot of losing strategies had been tried to get him more interested in school and reading, with the net effect of tuning him out instead of turning him on. That's the trouble with losing strategies—you don't just tread water; as in football, poor strategies mean you lose ground instead of gaining it. The first big losing strategy was Earl's notion that educating his son was the job of the school: Why should he interfere where he didn't belong? This kind of thinking is common among parents regardless of their background—rich, poor, well educated, or uneducated. These parents feel that since they've paid their tax dollars, it's now the school's problem to get their kid to perform. So they withdraw. Often, like Earl, parents who employ this losing strategy opt out of discussions about reading, book reports, projects, plays, anything concerned with school. They just don't want to be bothered; it's not their job.

The parents' motives can be selfish (they don't want to spend time talking about school) or selfless (they honestly believe they will screw up the teachers' good work if they get involved). But the result is the same: The kids perceive that their parents don't place much emphasis on school performance, and the kids act accordingly. Why should they worry about school if their parents don't care? Often, whatever the parents do care about supplants school as the primary focus in the kids' minds. In Jeremy's case, he had picked up years ago that his father valued mechanical aptitude and hated academics. So Jeremy had emulated these values, to his own disservice. Now that Jeremy's mother wasn't around, her proeducation influence was gone, and Jeremy never thought much about "the importance of learning" anymore. Actually, he tried not think about his mother and things that reminded him of her because it was so painful for him. He identified more and more with the parent he lived with, Earl, and his schoolwork became insignificant to both of them. The lesson of this story is that parents should remember that they transmit their beliefs and values to their children, even if they don't realize it. So Earl's strategy of staying out of the school thing because he didn't know how to help was becoming more and more detrimental to Jeremy.

The second big losing strategy consisted of Earl's failure to create a more regimented environment for Jeremy after school. Earl thought it was best for his son to play with his friends for positive feelings and support, reasoning that Jeremy was an only child who had lost the person in the world he was closest to. Rather than enroll Jeremy in after-school programs or activities that would challenge him, Earl had decided to "let him be a kid." Again, Earl's failure to create a school-oriented environment was due partly to his own attitude about school. But Jeremy ended up with far too much unstructured time for a twelve-year-old boy. Predictably, he used this time—almost four hours a day!—to eat junk food, to play video games, and occasionally to play with his model cars. Earl didn't want to be too tough on Jeremy, didn't want to force him to grow up too fast, wanted him to play and be carefree. But the self-esteem Jeremy lost as he fell behind in school and failed to accomplish things like the other kids meant that he was *anything but* a carefree kid. The key to understanding why strategy number two was a loser is to remember that more regimentation and discipline about schoolwork at home is often a positive thing for children: It helps them develop good working habits and feelings of confidence and self-efficacy.

The absence of structured after-school activities meant that Jeremy often felt distracted, directionless, and unfocused at home in his empty apartment after school. When Jeremy was lonely, or confused, or sad, he turned to his favorite cure: the video game. It was always there waiting for him, it didn't talk back or give him a hard time, and he didn't have to work to have fun with it. Plus, Jeremy scored higher and cannibalized more simians than any of his friends. With his mom gone and his dad exhausted and overworked, Jeremy turned inward, losing himself in the virtual reality of simian invaders and other games that define "fun" as killing, maiming, or (for the lightweights and faint of heart) torturing other living creatures. As his father, it was up to Earl to call a halt to this addiction. Left untreated, the video game junkie Jeremy was becoming was bound to slip deeper into simian hell.

The next big losing strategy had to do with Earl's self-consciousness about his own lackluster performance in school. Earl had never gotten over the embarrassment he'd felt in school. Earl's parents had never helped him—in fact they had ridiculed him and worsened the problem—so Earl had no positive experiences to draw on as a model for how he should behave with his son. Because of this, he evaded Jeremy whenever he thought Jeremy might ask him to help in preparing for a test or writing a book report. Earl didn't want to look dumb in front of his son: He wanted to be seen as the strong and capable father he was, as a positive authority figure in his son's life. So he shied away from helping Jeremy, even though the boy desperately needed assistance and positive reinforcement.

Earl had been raised to believe that saying "I don't know" is a sign of weakness, especially in a man. Rather than allow his son to hear him say so, Earl pretended that he knew the answers but didn't have the time or energy to help. The effect of this losing strategy was to make Jeremy feel that his father cared not an *iota* about Jeremy's work in school, that schoolwork was not worth getting excited about, and that to please his father Jeremy would have to turn his attention elsewhere—to classic Mustangs, for example, which really got Earl pumped up! When Jeremy talked about cars and displayed his ever-increasing knowledge base, he and his father bonded like Siamese twins.

The other negative effect of Earl's embarrassment

about his own performance in school was that he taught Jeremy that (a) it's best never to say "I don't know" or "Can you explain that?" and (b) it's natural to react to poor performance by *withdrawing from the challenge* and becoming embarrassed and defensive about it. Even though Earl never directly *verbalized* these lessons to his son, he couldn't possibly have taught them more thoroughly than by his consistent example. Jeremy had learned to look down, avoid questions, and give up when it came to school tasks. But the same kid could design and build his own model cars, tenaciously search out every piece of information he needed with no outside assistance, and see the projects through to completion. Jeremy had learned to back off from *school* challenges—but not from all challenges. When he cared about a subject he was amazingly competent; this meant that there was hope for Jeremy, if only he could learn once again to care about school.

The next big bust of a strategy concerned the amazing Mrs. Smyth. She was a teacher sent down from the heavens—the kind all of us want for our kids. And on top of this, she liked Jeremy and wanted to help. But Earl hadn't made good use of the valuable resource Mrs. Smyth represented. She had offered several times to place Jeremy in the after-school groups she supervised, but Earl had said no. She had offered to work after school with Jeremy twice a week for an hour on reading, but Earl thought this was overkill and wondered why she was so upset about his son when he was such a great kid. Mrs. Smyth had also suggested a special supplemental reading class for Jeremy that would give him extra time in a small group with a good instructor, but again Earl had said no, thinking that this would stigmatize his son and make the other kids think he was dumb. Earl had hated being taken out of class for extra help, and he wasn't going to unleash that embarrassment on his boy. So there was a whole group of losing strategies involving Earl's failure to take Mrs. Smyth's suggestions: Although Earl thought he was protecting Jeremy, he was filling his scorecard with zeros instead.

Another big losing strategy consisted of Earl's avoidance of all teacher-parent conferences and parents' day at science and book fairs. Earl thought it would be best not to make a fuss and embarrass his son: If he went to the science fair and Jeremy's project was lousy, it would be embarrassing! If he went to the book fair and Jeremy had trouble deciding which books to get because he couldn't read well, it would be *really* embarrassing! And those parent-teacher conferences weren't necessary: Jeremy wasn't flunking out, and Earl thought the school should be in charge of Jeremy's education. Plus, he knew nothing about succeeding in school—he'd mess it up even worse if he talked to Jeremy's teachers. Then every teacher would think even less of Jeremy because they'd know that his father was dumber than he was!

But, again, to Jeremy a difference picture was being filled in as Earl connected the dots: A picture of a father who didn't place much emphasis on schoolwork and who didn't think his son's science project was important. True, it wasn't one of the very best projects, but it was quite innovative. (Jeremy had made a diorama that showed how people on earth see the phases of the moon. Unlike many other kids, whose parents had basically built their science projects for them, Jeremy had built his own, and it was good. Too bad his father never found out about it!) The sad point is that Earl wanted what was best for his son, but he used one losing strategy after another. But there is hope for parents like Earl and kids like Jeremy—all they need are a few solid *winning* strategies in place of all those well-intentioned but losing ones.

The best effect of any book is that it excites the reader to self-activity.
—THOMAS CARLYLE

WINNING STRATEGIES

The single biggest winning strategy for this family is for Earl to deal with his own past issues concerning school, and admit to himself that school is important and should be the center of his son's life. There is no winning for Jeremy the way things stand now. Despite Earl's desire to be a good father, he is single-handedly halting Jeremy's progress in school. Regardless of whether Earl was a complete flop in school or only a partial flop, it is now Jeremy's turn and he should be doing his absolute best. So the first step is for Earl to change the way he thinks about school and start making it a daily priority in the household. There has to be an emphasis on schoolwork, reading, and school responsibility; a disciplined environment that encourages and supports daily reading; and a strong parental influence stressing reading as a central and meaningful life skill. (Yes, this means the video games should definitely be shelved!)

First, Earl must make decisions based on the premise that *school comes first* in a twelve-year-old's life.

He should enroll Jeremy in the after-school reading program and the supplemental reading class. Earl should arrange for Jeremy's after-school time to be filled with school-related, challenging activities, although not necessarily always *academic* activities: Jeremy could participate in sports, or join the drama group and be part of the play (as Sharene wanted him to). Maybe Jeremy won't be a gifted actor, and maybe remembering the lines would be too tough to start out—but with his exceptional mechanical and creative ability he could help make scenery and props for the play. All of these activities would help Jeremy feel more like he belonged at school. He'd make more friends and become more integrated into his new environment. And joining the after-school reading programs would be perfect for him: Mrs. Smyth used these programs to stress reading for pleasure, so Jeremy could try books about cars or even books about video games or hackers and read as many of them as he wanted.

The next step for Earl is to spend at least a half hour, three or four times a week, reading and going over schoolwork with his son. Earl found time for other, less important pursuits such as watching baseball and hockey games; he could make time for Jeremy. Earl could start by just quizzing Jeremy straight from the textbooks where the answers are printed at the end of the book—this way, the fact that Earl doesn't know the answers would not be a problem. Earl could go over Jeremy's homework with him by asking Jeremy to read it aloud: This would help Jeremy's reading and improve his writing, give Jeremy more self-confidence about speaking up, and let Jeremy know that his father cares, all without forcing the issue of exactly which answers are right and wrong. If Earl doesn't know the answers, he should learn to say so. Kids realize that a lot of what they're taught in school is rarely used in adult life. So, as a parent, if you don't know the answer, just say you used to know but you've forgotten—Jeremy didn't care that his father had forgotten the right answers as long as Earl helped and they looked up the answers together.

The key here is for Earl to shift his focus away from the facts that he does or doesn't know, and concentrate instead on the process of learning, reading, writing, and doing homework. The facts come and go. (How many specific facts can you remember about the Louisiana Purchase? How many characters can you remember from *Uncle Tom's Cabin?*) But the experience of learning how to read and integrate information, how to find answers to questions, and how to evaluate what is being learned is still with you, just as it is still with Earl. Earl has a responsible managerial position in a large company—he knows how to locate information, make decisions, and evaluate outcomes. He knows the process of learning and using what he has learned. So even though Earl doesn't know all the precise details of what Jeremy is studying, he does know how to help his son by showing how to get information and use it.

Tonight at the dinner table, Earl should intercept Jeremy before he disappears into simian city and ask him to bring out his books and lay them out while Earl does the dishes and straightens up the kitchen. As Earl occupies himself with his chores, Jeremy can work through some questions with the aid of his father. Earl doesn't have to be staring over Jeremy's shoulder every minute—he can be paying bills, doing his own paperwork, whatever. The significant change is that Jeremy is expected to read and do schoolwork every evening at the dining table, making the activity a part of the family's daily routine, instead of being allowed to vanish into his bedroom to play mind-numbing video games. Jeremy should also be expected to spend some time on his own in his room, *working* (not playing video games!) to develop the habit of concentrating alone on his work, while knowing that his father is available to help if needed.

Then there's the issue of all those school-related events Earl has been avoiding. It's time Earl realized that he has to go to at least some, even if he can't stay for the entire time due to work commitments. An hour spent at the science fair would allow Earl to show that his son's project is important to him, regardless of whether it is one of the strongest or one of the weakest exhibits. In fact, Jeremy's is just as good as the other kids' projects—and Earl might be pleasantly surprised to learn this! A conference with Jeremy's teachers would put Earl in touch with what Jeremy does and doesn't need help with. Plus, some of the teachers who are being tough on Jeremy might ease up if they knew the situation at home. And Earl should plan on attending the school play and clapping loudly for his son; even if his contribution is limited to making sets, it is significant.

The winning resource represented by Mrs. Smyth is too good for Earl to pass up. He should go to see her immediately and express his sincere thanks for her kindness and interest in his son. Mrs. Smyth would be happy to speak to Earl for ten minutes a week to fill him in on Jeremy's progress—and to give him specific suggestions for things to do at home that would help Jeremy. But Earl has to call and listen. And Mrs. Smyth could learn from Earl about Jeremy's real loves in life (other than Sharene, that is). She could pick a couple of books Jeremy would love, and work with Jeremy on them at the after-school reading hour. Mrs. Smyth and the school librarian would be well able to select books that would provide Jeremy with the academic development he needs while still keeping him interested. The result will be that Jeremy's attitude about school will begin to change as school begins to take a front seat in his life, and as the information he learns in school starts to have significance for him.

Another winning strategy for the home environment has to do with books themselves. At present there are few books around, so Jeremy got the message that books weren't important. So Earl's mission today is to take Jeremy to the library to get an armful of books. There are plenty of books about subjects Jeremy is interested in, like cars, building things, project ideas, how-to titles, video game designers (if Jeremy just can't get that stuff out of his system!), etc. There are also books of stories for kids Jeremy's age—stories about children who have lost a parent to death or divorce, or children who are starting life anew in a new school and city. These sorts of stories would strike a chord and resonate with Jeremy's experience. The librarian would be able to help Jeremy find some of these books.

The school reading Jeremy does should stress academics, but the home reading can be more focused on his personal interests. Earl might also want to challenge Jeremy to build a special model car that isn't well documented and let Jeremy search out the information he needs at the library. Or, Earl could challenge Jeremy to create his own idea for a video game based on information he could find in biographies or stories about successful game designers. These challenges would get Jeremy motivated to find information on his own and would give him experience in using the library as a tool. And most librarians would be glad to point Jeremy in the right direction and give him needed support to get started.

Tomorrow's mission is for Earl and Jeremy to add the library or the bookstore to their regular itinerary of stops every Saturday. It doesn't mean they have to spend a lot of money: Jeremy should get used to spending time in the bookstore, just browsing. Next birthday, Earl could give his son a gift certificate from the bookstore—and when it's Earl's birthday, he could ask Jeremy to get a book for him. Earl should remember to read some books himself, out in the living room, instead of always picking up the remote and vegging out on the sofa. Maybe the two could plan a road trip for school vacation, using travel guides and other printed material . . . or maybe they could plan to visit some local landmarks together in their new home state, learning a little about California's history by reading about it and visiting interesting places. The same old sedentary pattern is doing neither of them any good, and it's not helping them rebuild their lives after the loss of Jeremy's mother. It's time to get up and get out into the world, and get enthusiastic about a few new activities. As Jeremy's grandmother used to say, "Move a muscle, change a thought."

Other winning strategies involve linking events that Earl and Jeremy can attend together with later *reading* about the events. Next weekend the two could consider an antique and classic car show, followed by a trip to the bookstore or library to get a book on classic cars. Even if the book is mostly pictures, it's a start, and it will show Jeremy that books aren't the enemy. Soon Jeremy will be ready for books with a bit more substance because he has begun to learn the *habit* of sitting down with a book instead of in front of a video game. Over time, as Jeremy comes to enjoy reading, his choice of reading materials can be broadened. Of course, reading for school should be stressed: Jeremy is reading well behind the other children in his class and his school performance must be improved. But Jeremy can also do out-of-school reading on subjects of interest to him and reap significant improvements in school reading as a reward. The key is to start Jeremy out on reading that is nonthreatening and that he will enjoy— then later move on to choices designed to enlarge his experiences with books and broaden his reading choices.

Maybe Jeremy would like to make a scrapbook showing the progression of a major project that he and his father could undertake together, like building their own model (or actual!) car. Scrapbooks entail reading and writing, even though Jeremy won't see it this way and won't perceive it as Dad forcing him to do school-work in his spare time. Another winning idea is for Jeremy to be challenged to create his own Trivial Pursuit board game, all about cars and sports and the other things he and his father love. (He could even design a Trivial Pursuit game based on video game characters and ideas from the games, if this turns out to be the only way to get him excited about the project.) Jeremy would be responsible for writing up the game cards and designing the game board and rules. Earl and Jeremy could play the game with Jeremy's new friends and challenge them to add to the deck of game cards. And perhaps Jeremy would be excited about receiving a few magazines about cars and gadget building: These subscriptions are usually not expensive, and since it's reading that seems nothing like school, Jeremy won't likely throw it down in disgust. The library also has stacks of magazines on topics Jeremy likes—if he gets really interested, he can even pore over back issues piled up to his eyeballs. The happy side effect here is that Jeremy will be learning to enjoy the library and use it to locate information valuable to him. Again, if necessary, magazines about video games could be used to induce Jeremy to read, but only in moderation, since the real goal is to break him of his unhealthy video game habit.

Another winning strategy for this family involves writing to pen pals. Since Jeremy and his father have recently moved across the country, leaving behind much of their extended family, Jeremy might be enticed into writing letters to the people left behind. Maybe the relatives and friends back in New Jersey would like to receive copies of Jeremy's new scrapbook (made on a color photocopier at a local copy shop). Maybe Jeremy might even like to design a sheet of special car-buff stationery, have it photocopied, and use it for letters. If Earl called some of Jeremy's old friends back home, he might be able to get them to start the ball rolling by writing to Jeremy . . . whatever it takes to get words coming off the kid's pen!

If the family owns a personal computer (which of course is another way kids like Jeremy play video games), it is also possible that Jeremy's interest in video games could be transferred to a healthier interest in computers themselves and how they work. This would have to be done in moderation, with close monitoring by Earl, to keep Jeremy from trading one addiction for another. Possible healthy uses of a computer for Jeremy include reading and navigating through books on CD-ROM, and access to an electronic-mail bulletin board or to Worldwide Web information files that Jeremy could read (under Earl's supervision). If the kid is so steeped in technology that he balks at the idea of words printed on paper, it's possible that words on a computer screen would get him psyched up to read faster than traditional books.

Little by little, as Jeremy reads here and there, to himself and aloud, he will redefine his self-image, seeing himself now as a good reader who likes school. As Jeremy gets more involved in school activities and becomes more comfortable with himself, he will begin to see himself as a good student, especially if his father is cheering on his progress and sharing in his accomplishments. Jeremy won't care whether his dad memorizes the details of the Louisiana Purchase (I've forgotten all of them too); what does matter is that Earl places a value on Jeremy's performance in school.

The unfortunate thing about Jeremy's story is that its main theme is very common. Often, one parent or individual in the household takes responsibility for creating a school-oriented environment. When this parent or other person moves, leaves, or dies, the environment crumbles. This same pattern occurs when there are two parents who work fifty hours a week and a great baby-sitter or child-care provider who does his or her best to help the children with school. One day, circumstances intervene and the child-care provider is out of the kids' lives. Then the pyramid collapses, because kids need reinforcement from their caretakers to continue to place an emphasis on school. I know one family who depended so completely on their nanny to teach their children and prepare them for school that when the nanny had to move (because her husband was relocated), the family moved too! The point is that regardless of who creates the school-oriented environment at home, it is an essential ingredient of a child's winning recipe as a student. Teachers can help, but it is in the home night after night that the habits of working for and succeeding in school are forged.

Most important, Jeremy's life will get a size larger and his interests and motivation will grow in response to more home discipline and more challenges both in school and in his other activities. Jeremy loses himself in the isolating world of video games because he is bored and confused by the pressures and worries in his life, and he does not have the wisdom or experience to choose healthier pursuits that would ultimately be more fun. Jeremy does not know how to handle his problems; he needs direction and support from his father. Life can be tough, especially at age twelve; children today often face more pressures than they should. The cure for kids like Jeremy is to show them, through *positive example* and through *positive, reinforcing, supportive action*, that there are more rewarding ways to spend time than by playing video games. The lesson may not sink in at first, but whether or not the child *sees* why video games are bad, he will learn the lesson by *feeling* the positive differences in his life soon enough.

Curing a video game junkie isn't easy, but it can be done. The key is to remember that arguing with kids and explaining why video games are Lucifer incarnate probably won't solve the problem. If the child has too much unstructured time, the video game will continue to be chosen to fill it. Instead of developing laryngitis reciting the evils of video game addiction, parents should take direct and positive *action* to *show* their kids the alternatives. If parents and children have fun exploring other ways to spend time, kids will get excited about real-life action and experiences instead of virtual reality. Video games will be replaced by books and other healthy activities if parents set the example by showing and sharing with kids an active lifestyle that reveals video games as the waste of time they are.

When I get a little money, I buy books; and if any is left, I buy food and clothes.
—DESIDERIUS ERASMUS (1465–1536)

MORALS OF JEREMY'S STORY

How to Get and Keep Kids Reading

• If you didn't enjoy or do well in reading as a child, don't advertise this fact to *your* child. He might think there's no point in trying to do better if you couldn't— or he might think you turned out okay without reading, so why bother to try?

• If you didn't do well with reading or school, remember that you can still help your child succeed with reading and school today.

• Create an environment for reading and school success by encouraging your child to read and do homework every day as a part of the family routine. Set a time and make a place so that you child feels supported in these activities.

- Listen when teachers tell you about your child's needs and make an effort to try teachers' suggestions.
- Recognize and thank teachers directly, and also compliment them to the principal, when they go out of their way to help your child.
- Use hobbies and activities your child loves to lure him into reading—show how, with the right book, reading can become a part of any activity
- Participate in reading with your child about a topic or interest the two of you share.
- Expect your child to succeed in school, and *never* use your past weaknesses as a justification for your child's present performance.
- Make use of school activities like reading groups and library study groups to put your child in contact with others who are working to improve their reading.
- Encourage your child to be involved in school and outside-of-school projects that involve reading, especially reading aloud.
- Realize that changes in family dynamics occur when a parent or caretaker leaves. If that person helped the child with reading, you or someone else must now take up the slack.
- Reward any effort or gain in performance to build your child's confidence and belief in his reading ability—and to reinforce the idea that through *effort*, performance will improve.
- Respond to a child's immersion in video or computer games with *understanding* and *action*: First, *understand* that he plays the games because he believes they are more fun than the other options for spending his

time; second, take *action* by showing and sharing with your child alternative ways of spending time that are likely to be more rewarding to him. Stick with him and support the transition to these other activities until they become pleasurable habits.

• As you work with your child to wean him from video and computer games, *watch your child closely* and *limit time* spent on these games. Work gradually to replace video games with other, healthier pursuits.

CHAPTER FIVE

STEPPING TO A
DIFFERENT DRUMMER:
KIM'S STORY

One could get a first-class education from a shelf of books five feet long.
—CHARLES WILLIAM ELIOT (when President of Harvard University)

Temples fall, statues decay, mausoleums perish, eloquent phrases declaimed are forgotten, but good books are immortal.
—WILLIAM TECUMSEH VERNON

Kim could hear her grandmother's conversation drifting up the back stairway. "Good work, Ronny, good work. Keep going . . . what's 14 times 69? . . . 173 divided by 47? . . ." *It was like being forced to endure math class twice a day,* Kim thought as she groaned out loud and turned up her music. Kim was fourteen, and in her first year of high school. At the moment she was doing what she liked best: working on her painting of birds sitting on the outside banister, with cherry blossoms in the background. But somehow the tranquillity of the scene was spoiled by her grandmother and little brother reciting math equations. "Kim! Turn that music down! Your brother is trying to work!" her grandmother yelled up the stairs. *What do you call what I'm*

139

doing? Kim thought, lowering the volume. The sound of droning math calculations floated back in. Finally, Kim gave up, closed her box of watercolors, and put down her brush. "Dammit!" she muttered, as her grandmother yelled for her to come downstairs and help with dinner.

Kim stalked down the stairs and confronted her grandmother. "Nanna, I was trying to paint! It's hard to do any creative work around here with all this stupid noise. Why can't you and Ronny work in the other room, or at least keep it down . . . or better yet, why can't Ronny do his own homework?"

Nanna glared at her, handing Kim a bunch of carrots. "This is nonsense, Kim! Ronny is doing important work. You're upstairs wasting time, as usual. You're just jealous because Ronny enjoys his schoolwork so much. Now wash and peel these!" Kim sighed superloud and began preparing the carrots.

At that moment her older sister Alison burst in, dressed like a bag lady on a New York City subway. Nanna blanched, sat down, and clutched at her chest. "Alison, you look like a street person! Such a beautiful girl, but you make yourself look like garbage. I can't take the stress of you girls. You have closets filled with perfectly beautiful, expensive clothes, but you dress in thrift-store rags!"

Alison looked at Kim and smiled. "Looks great, doesn't it?" she asked.

"Primo," Kim answered, laughing as she peeled the carrots.

Just then Ronny interrupted by waving his paper through the air, saying, "Hey! People are trying to work around here. Can you all *please* stop arguing? Who cares what they wear! I'm trying to get ready for a math test tomorrow."

Nanna smiled at Ronny, then looked up at the girls and barked, "All right, Kim, get those carrots cooking. Alison, set the table. Ronny, keep working. Your mom and dad will be home soon—we've got to get dinner ready."

Kim boiled water for the carrots and started humming to herself. It was a haunting Irish melody she had just learned on the flute. She rehearsed the piece in her mind as she stirred the rice in time to the beat. Then the front door opened, and Kim tensed as she heard her mother in the front hallway. Kim dreaded her mother's arrival because every night it was the same story: Her mother would praise Ronny for working so hard and getting such good grades, praise Alison for winning second place in the science fair, then look at Kim and ask how she was doing in English class. Kim would talk about getting the lead role in the school play, writing a new flute composition for the next recital, or being chosen to do the artwork for the freshman yearbook, but her mother would cut her off and ask about English and her other courses. Why couldn't her mother get excited about what Kim really cared about? she wondered, as her mother walked into the kitchen and kissed Ronny.

Kim's mother, Janet, sorted through the mail as she mechanically recapped her schedule for the day. Janet was an attorney specializing in family law. She put in ten-hour days at minimum and expected no less from her children. Every night she would drill her kids on what they had accomplished that day, how they were doing in school, and how much homework they'd been assigned. Janet respected good grades more than anything else—when the children did well in school, the world was golden, but when one of them slipped up in a core subject, Janet tightened down like a warden. As Janet began to describe one of the stickier divorce cases she was handling, she told Kim to stop humming and listen.

"Maybe you'd learn something if you'd just pay attention, Kim. Law is a wonderful career. You seem to think it's a meaningless way for me to be spending my life, but I assure you my clients wouldn't agree with you." Kim didn't even bother answering; she continued dishing out the food as Alison brought the plates to the table. Kim's father, Donald, wasn't home yet and probably wouldn't make it for dinner. Donald was a professor in the English department of a large university, and he outworked even his wife. "Better leave a plate in the oven for Daddy," Alison said. "He hasn't been home before eight o'clock one night this week!"

The family sat down at the table and Ronny started stabbing at food like a prison-camp survivor. Nanna finally took off her apron and joined them after rounding up her husband, who was asleep in front of a quiz show on television. Nanna announced, "Grace!" and the family methodically clasped their hands as Nanna ran through the usual routine. Then it was open season, and Janet started firing her usual battery of questions. Kim looked down, answered the questions directed to her in monosyllables, and finished her meal as fast as she could. Then she went back up to her room to finish her painting, as Alison went on and on *and on* about her physics class and the interesting lab exercises they were doing.

Janet helped clear the table, then went to her bedroom to change. Her head ached, her feet ached, and she felt worn out. It had been such a long day. Just then Donald came up the stairs and into the bedroom, where he collapsed on the bed, still in his outdoor jacket.

"Why don't you change your clothes, honey? You'll feel better," Janet said.

"I'm too beat to move!" answered Donald, kicking off his shoes. "How are you doing? How's the new divorce case going? What's new with the kids?"

Janet filled him in on the details of her day, then walked into the bathroom to draw a tub. "You know, Don, I'm really worried about Kim. Alison is headed for a first-rate college—she's going to be a doctor or a scientist, and I have no doubt she'll succeed at whatever she tries. Ronny is brilliant; he's been moved into an accelerated reading program and is doing work at the high-school level even though he's only in sixth grade. Both of them spend every spare minute reading everything they're assigned at school and then reading extra books on everything under the sun! They're learning every chance they get.

"But then there's Kim. All she cares about lately is her music, acting in school plays, and painting the same types of pictures over and over. She's getting by in her classes because she's so bright, but she does only the minimum necessary to get an A or an A-minus. She spends as little time as possible studying, and when she's done preparing for school she never opens a book! Sooner or later her lack of enthusiasm for learning is going to catch up with her; her natural ability will take her only so far. I don't know what to do to help her! In some ways she's the most talented of our children, but I'm afraid she'll never make the most of her gifts if she doesn't learn to love the *process* of learning."

Donald looked concerned. As an English professor, he loved books and spent most of his working life immersed in the study of the printed word. Janet also read extensively and depended on books to do her job. The couple had been married for eighteen years, during which they had accumulated quite an impressive personal library. They had tried to raise all three of their children to love learning in every form, but especially to love books: They gave their kids books for every birthday and holiday, and they read widely themselves and talked often about books with their children. Plus, Donald had written four books himself. So the thought that Kim was somehow turning off to scholarly work and learning was deeply disappointing to him.

"Maybe we've been pushing her too hard," Donald said. "Her grades are *A*s to high *B*s, and she's involved in music and acting as extracurricular activities. It's true that she doesn't enjoy talking about academics like Ronny and Alison, and it's true that she does the minimum to get an *A,* but at least she usually *gets* the *A*! She may grow into a more academic mind-set as she goes through high school. She'll be more challenged as the courses get more advanced, and out of pride and a desire to keep up with Alison and Ronny she'll keep on fighting for *A*s. I think she's just a free spirit: She's got her own muse. I don't think we should keep on nagging her or we'll turn her off more!"

"I don't know, Don," Janet said. "She's at a critical age. Either she's excited about learning and doors open, or she's not and they close. She's in high school now, and her transcript is all-important to what college she'll go to. I don't think we can do too much to try to help her at this stage of the game. If we lose her now, she'll wind up in ten years as a frustrated, poverty-stricken artist living on the street. It's embarrassing. I'm going to visit the school again and talk to a couple of her teachers."

"When are you going to find the time for that—between hearings?" her husband shot back, as he headed downstairs to eat his desiccated dinner.

The next day Janet placed a few calls to Kim's teachers during a rare break in her workday. Mr. Wong was thrilled with Kim's performance in vocal and music classes, but predictably he was the only teacher who was so blanketedly positive. The others were a bit more measured. "Kim's a solid student," Ms. Harley, the English teacher, told Janet. "She does her work on time and she does quite a competent job. She's generally in the *B*-plus range or higher. But on the other hand, she doesn't seem to love school the way Alison did. She talks about becoming an artist or a musician, and once in a while she cuts class to sit outdoors and draw charcoal sketches of birds and trees. Kim's a bright girl with a lot to offer; she just seems a bit turned off to school right now." Janet replaced the receiver, having received confirmation of what she had suspected. There was no need to make the trip to school to hear it again. What worried Janet most was Kim's lack of spark for things academic. It seemed that Kim was just biding her time until school was over. Janet got a pain in her stomach when she imagined Kim becoming a musician or artist. *God help us,* she thought.

Unaware that at that very moment her mother was getting bent out of shape, Kim was enjoying herself at play rehearsal. She loved working with the other kids on the play, which this term was *Carousel*. Kim had a beautiful voice with great projection, and Mr. Wong felt lucky to have her as a student. Kim sat reading through her lines. Her mind wandered when she saw her English teacher, Ms. Harley, walking down the hall. *Why can't Mom just let up for a while?* she thought. Kim got good grades. She couldn't help it if she got sick of that heavy academic stuff; she couldn't wait until she graduated and it was over. Three more years of school and she'd be out. As far as she was concerned, Alison and Ronny could go to school till they died if they wanted; but Kim was ready to see the world. She was already planning to travel to South America and Australia as soon as she was old enough to go without her parents. She knew they wouldn't approve, but in a few years they'd have no more say. It wasn't like she wanted them to pay for college or anything, Kim reasoned. She just wanted to be out on her own.

The bell rang, jolting Kim back to reality, and she groaned audibly. "What's the matter?" her friend Sam asked.

"I hate English class—I hate the way Ms. Harley teaches it! It's supposed to be beautiful to read poetry and great literature. It's supposed to be something you experience, something that enriches you, but she makes it a chore. She picks such bogus stuff for us to read, then she tests us like a drill sergeant on all the meaningless details, like the intricacies of the plot and the names of all the characters. I can't stand it. It seems so pointless."

Sam laughed. "Why don't you tell her, Kim?"

"Oh, God, I couldn't do that or she'd give me a *C!*" Kim responded.

"Well, how would you teach it then, if you were in charge?"

"I'd make it a journey through the soul," Kim answered, throwing her head back and lifting her arms into a yoga position, as Sam howled, grabbed Kim's hand, and pulled her up out of her seat.

She barely made it to English class on time, which was typical. Kim was often the last student through the door. Ms. Harley was handing out a booklet of some sort and announcing, "Okay, time for a surprise test! Close your books and put them under your desks. You'll have forty minutes to finish. Don't start until I say so." Kim clenched her teeth and whispered her mother's least-favorite word five times to herself. She hadn't finished *The Jungle*, which was what the class had been reading this week. She'd found it too depressing, so she'd just stopped reading after the second chapter. She had meant to buy the Monarch Notes because she knew Ms. Harley loved to give surprise tests, especially on long books with lots of details—but she hadn't gotten around to it yet. Kim took a deep breath and opened the test.

Forty minutes seemed like ten to most of the class, as they wrote fast and furiously to finish the long test on time. But to Kim, forty minutes seemed like forty hours, because she didn't know eighty percent of the material. If the test had contained essay questions she could have written something and fudged a lot more. But it was mostly short-answer stuff about who did what, when, and where. With that kind of test, either you read the whole book carefully or you didn't. *Oh well*, Kim thought, *it's only one test!* She promised herself that she'd be ready for the next one. Then her mind wandered to the play again. She loved starring opposite Sam, who was one of the school studs. Lately, play rehearsal, vocal and music class, and art class were the only things she enjoyed at school. At that moment, Ms. Harley interrupted Kim's fantasy about Sam by picking up Kim's paper. Kim's fate was sealed, and the class was dismissed.

When Ms. Harley looked over the papers that night, she was disturbed by what she perceived as a downward trend in Kim's performance. She had pulled Kim's paper out of the pile and read it through. The fact that Kim had barely glanced at the book was as obvious as a drunk in dance class. Ms. Harley wrote *C+* on the top of the test and added this comment: "Kim: The parts you read are represented well, but it seems as though you never got past chapter 2. Your grades have been slipping lately, and you aren't paying attention in class. You started out the term a solid *B+/A-* student, but your average is slipping. Please speak to me after class."

When Kim got the paper back two days later she stuffed it into her backpack without even reading Ms. Harley's comment. As class ended, she and Sam walked out the back door, heading for the cafeteria. Ms. Harley practically had a cow, and chased Kim right out into the hall. "Kim! Where are you going? You were supposed to see me after class!"

Kim looked surprised, which of course she was. "Sorry, Ms. Harley, I didn't realize," she said, following her teacher back into the classroom. Sam waved and said he'd catch up with her later.

Ms. Harley was infuriated now, realizing that Kim hadn't even bothered to read the comments she'd written. "Kim, I'm very concerned about your grades in my class. Don't you understand how important English class is when people evaluate your transcript? You're such a bright girl, and I know your parents encourage you and want you to do well so you can attend a good college. Why are you throwing it all away like this?" Kim tried to explain that school didn't matter to her as much as art, music, acting, and seeing the world. But Ms. Harley couldn't connect with these reasons, and she closed the conversation by saying she would call Kim's mother that afternoon.

Janet was in court and didn't get the message until the next day, but when she returned Ms. Harley's call she became deeply angry. She couldn't believe that Kim was slacking off like this; she had always done well in school, even if she didn't love it like her siblings did. At Janet's insistent urging (that bordered on begging), Ms. Harley agreed to let Kim read one extra book and take an extra test on it to replace her poor grade on this test. Janet prepared to confront Kim that evening; she was determined that Kim get an *A* on the makeup test. The first thing on Janet's agenda as she walked through the front door that night was to speak with Kim, which she did. Kim felt bad about her poor performance; after all, she was accustomed to getting mostly *A*s. She had intended to finish *The Jungle* over the weekend, she just hadn't had the time—and she obviously hadn't known about the surprise test.

Kim tried to be conciliatory with her mother, but the conversation broke down when Janet told her that she had to read *1984* over the weekend and take a makeup test on Monday. "But I have plans for the weekend!" Kim protested. "Why can't I have a week to read the book?"

"Because then you'll fall behind the rest of the class next week as they begin another book," her mother explained. "That's why you're supposed to read this extra book over the *weekend*—so you won't miss anything by doing it. The rest of the class won't be starting their next book yet."

Kim was dejected. "But I have play rehearsal, and a party tomorrow night with Sam, and other things to do!"

"I guess you should have budgeted your time more effectively," her mother answered, getting up to help serve dinner. "There will be no more discussion. You are grounded this weekend, and you will get at least an *A*-minus on this makeup test, or you will be grounded next weekend too!"

Kim couldn't believe what she was hearing. "I'm not a child, Mother! You can't treat me like this."

"Yes I can, Kim, as long as you're living under this roof! You will maintain your grades before you get to be in plays and vocal groups and before you paint another damn bird. Now let's close this subject, shall we? I don't want to ruin dinner for everyone."

Kim felt like she had been hit by a semi. Yes, she had screwed up one test, but big deal! Her grades were all *B*-pluses or better: Why should she be punished like this? She couldn't miss play rehearsal without hurting everyone else in the group. The play started in three weeks—it was too close to showtime to miss any rehearsals now. Plus, missing the party with Sam was unthinkable; she had walked on air for two days after he'd asked her. The party was a school function designed to integrate ninth graders into the school and make them more comfortable in the high-school environment. She couldn't imagine why her mother would want her to miss that. Kim knew she should have read the book; it was just that her other commitments took up too much time. She was willing to read *1984* and take the makeup test. But this reaction of her mother's was way off-base—she couldn't believe it. Kim vowed to get back at her mother somehow for the humiliation this punishment represented. *She just doesn't understand me,* Kim thought, realizing that she had absolutely no appetite for dinner that night.

I've never known any trouble that an hour's reading didn't assuage.
—MONTESQUIEU

Books are the collective memory of mankind.
—HERBERT BAILEY SMITH

THE PROBLEM

Kids like Kim are many parents' dream of the perfect child: She was generally very successful in school, she was talented and attractive, she had plenty of friends, she participated in extracurricular activities, she was helpful at home, and she was a friendly, outgoing young woman. True, she didn't finish *The Jungle* in time for the Friday afternoon surprise test, but this was her worst slip-up in several months. Put into perspective, Kim's story doesn't seem all that bad. Many parents would have considered themselves lucky to have a daughter as accomplished as Kim. But there was a lot going on beneath the surface in Kim's life; she was becoming progressively more turned off to school and alienated from her parents, especially from her mother. And when she had begun high school a few months ago, she had started to show a tendency to avoid academics and especially reading, which as a child and adolescent she had loved.

Janet and Donald were concerned about Kim's priorities and especially about her growing lack of academic focus and decline in reading. Yes, she read for school, but only the absolute minimum amount and in the absolute minimum time. Her antibook focus stood in sharp contrast to the behavior of her brother and sister, who read every chance they got. But even Sherlock Holmes couldn't have caught Kim with a book in hand. The problem in Kim's case was complex, and as usual it involved a lot more than just reading. Heading the problem list was her parents and their attitude toward their children's academic performance in general and reading in particular. Donald and especially Janet were education zealots who were neurotic and overly involved in their kids' academic lives: They believed that educational success was the be-all and end-all of life; the only real evidence for the existence of the civilized mind; the height to which everyone must aspire (though few would attain their level, of course). There's nothing wrong with stressing educational success with children; in fact, most children would read more and perform better in school if their parents emphasized education more heavily in the home. But just as taking too many vitamins can make you sick, too much pressure on kids to conform to parental values can be stifling and eventually alienating. Why were Kim's parents so extreme in their views?

Janet had met Don at a prestigious college when they were undergraduates. She had gone on to one of the top law schools in the country, while he had pursued a Ph.D. in English at a first-rate university. They married in the university chapel, surrounded by the accoutrements of the academic life they valued. To Janet and Donald, the academic life represented every value they wanted to instill in their children: the quest for knowledge and the love of learning, the intrinsic value of education, the belief that education makes all people equals, the belief that education is the only true route to success. Janet's hard work and long hours in her law practice and Donald's ten-hour days as the chair of his department were spent in furtherance of the couple's goals.

When their children were born, they spared no effort or expense to bring them up "right." They were read to from birth (and even before birth, since Janet had read that unborn babies pick up information from their mother's environment), taken to culturally valuable plays and movies, and educated at every possible moment. Janet hired the best nannies she could find—she even paid extra to get well-educated help. Dinnertable discussions in this household centered on academic questions and issues, and even when the children were young they were asked their opinions on world events, politics, racial issues, crime, health issues, you name it. The parents' goal was to create children with a tremendous mental capacity and knowledge base, superchildren who could do virtually anything they wanted.

Lest the family's home life sound completely stultifying, remember that Ronny and Alison had blossomed in this environment, at least at this stage in their lives. (Later on, however, it is possible that Ronny and Alison might begin to rebel much as Kim had; different children have different thresholds and reactions to extreme parental expectations.) Kim's brother and sister were tremendously bright children who were naturally gifted academically. The emphasis on learning and displaying knowledge fit Ronny and Alison's personalities well—they thought learning was fun and they loved showing what they knew at every opportunity. But Kim, the middle child, had always been different. At age seven she began to show sensitivity to the criticism and chiding that were typical in the family. Her feelings were more easily hurt than her siblings'. A spirited discussion at the dinner table struck Kim more as an argument. But Kim was bright, and at seven she loved school, reading, and learning, so her parents thought she was just more introverted and touchy than the others.

At age eleven, Kim began the gradual process of withdrawing from the family's typical dynamic. She started spending more time alone in her room rather than doing schoolwork and reading with her siblings in the dining room. Kim learned to play the flute and piano, started acting in school plays, and began to paint. As her artistic talents developed, she spent more time alone, although her grades were still excellent. But as Kim progressed through adolescence she spent less and less time with the family and more and more time in her bedroom engaged in creative pursuits.

How did her parents react? Things deteriorated to the point that Kim sometimes felt her mother was her archenemy. At fourteen, a high-school freshman, Kim was paying progressively less attention to her schoolwork and focusing more completely on creative activities. She was a talented artist, musician, and actress, but her parents were wise to worry about her increasing abandonment of academics. If Kim did decide to pursue a career in an artistic area she would still need solid high-school grades to get accepted into a good college. But Kim saw no reason to attend college at all anymore. It was one of those situations when the baby is thrown out with the bathwater—an example of an inappropriately extreme reaction on Kim's part.

As Kim withdrew, she stopped paying attention in class and she stopped reading. In this household, reading was something Kim identified with her parents and siblings—exactly the people from whom she was trying to differentiate herself. Janet and Donald were beside themselves with worry and anger. They saw their previously wonderful child throwing her life away; when Kim began to reject academics, her parents saw it as a direct rejection of them and their family values. And in a way, it was. This reluctant reading situation was different from most in that the parents seemed to have performed many of the individual steps correctly—they had created an environment that fosters reading and learning, albeit a highly pressured one focused squarely on academic success. This approach had worked reasonably well with two of their three kids, at least for the time being. But children like Kim are not uncommon in families that push reading like a military basic-training regimen, and their reluctance to read seems all the more tragic because of their natural high level of ability and past reading success.

As Janet and Donald panicked, they, and especially Janet, took immediate action to help their daughter. Unfortunately, they tried umpteen losing strategies, bearing out the observation that well-educated and academically oriented parents often can't find their way out of a paper bag with both ends cut when it comes to seeing the shortcomings of their own approaches.

He has only half learned the art of reading who has not added to it the even more refined accomplishments of skipping and skimming.
—ARTHUR BALFOUR

LOSING STRATEGIES

Janet applied her tenacious bulldog rip-'em-and-shred-'em lawyer logic to her problems with Kim. After all, she reasoned, Kim wasn't a kid any longer, and her entire future was being compromised by her stupidity. Janet may have had a point, but her confrontational and combative approach didn't make Kim eager to board the reading and schoolwork bus. The more Janet pushed, bit, and shook, the more Kim withdrew and the more spiteful and angry she became.

Brilliant idea number one was Janet's decision to ground Kim for the entire weekend because of her poor grade on one unannounced test. The situation deserved attention, but Janet's reaction was extreme. Kim had an honest commitment to Mr. Wong (the play director) and the other performers, and forcing her to miss play rehearsal was counterproductive. First, it taught Kim that commitments made to other people could be sacrificed easily as long as there was a reason. Second, it taught Kim that her mother did not value what meant most to Kim: her artistic side, the long hours spent working on her play performance, her feelings of identification and belonging with Mr. Wong and with other students. Third, it more firmly established reading in Kim's mind as a dreaded chore—obviously not a desirable result. Viewed dispassionately, Kim's failure to finish *The Jungle* on time could be seen as a sign that she needed help in establishing priorities and budgeting her time more effectively (and who doesn't, especially at fourteen?). But Janet defined the problem as how to force Kim to read more *this instant*, rather than how to *redevelop Kim's love of reading*. So Janet blew it, big-time.

Brilliant idea number two was related to brilliant idea number one: Janet didn't allow Kim to attend the freshman class party she had been so excited about. Again, this was an overly punitive reaction to Kim's slipup. By forcing Kim to stay home Saturday night, her mother succeeded only in stirring up more resentment and feelings of alienation. Kim's distancing from academic subjects could have been offset by her beginning to feel more involved in school. Up until now Kim had felt like a bit of an outsider in her new school, with the exception of her drama and music work with Mr. Wong. The party that Saturday was planned by the school principal and teachers as one way to help the freshman kids get to know one another and their teachers in a more informal situation than daily classes. In the past, these parties had helped kids see the school as a more hospitable environment, and their teachers as less like clones of Attila the Hun. But Kim missed the party and the positive experience it could have represented. She spent the time playing the flute and watching television; she would rather have had a root canal than read a book that night!

Brilliant idea number three was Janet and Donald's decision to limit Kim's artistic endeavors to allow her more time for schoolwork in core subjects and for out-of-school reading. From the parents' perspective, Kim was simply spending too much time on all that bohemian stuff. As parents, they had to intervene to redirect their daughter's attention. New rules were made and imposed, such as, "Kim must spend two hours every weekday doing homework and reading at the dinner table with her siblings"; "Kim will not practice flute after dinner"; "Kim will not paint at home on weeknights; she will paint only in art class at school"; and "Kim will read for one hour every weekday and report her results and progress on a chart taped to her door."

From the parents' perspective, these rules seemed reasonable and in Kim's best interest. Trouble was, they were too restrictive and too extreme. Children like Kim don't bow easily to authority; attempting to force them to change major parts of their personalities simply will not work. Kim's parents were able to police how she spent her time, but they were not causing any positive attitude change: In fact, they were creating the most negative attitude change possible! Research has shown that a positive attitude toward reading is the single greatest predictor of time spent reading outside of school. Now that Kim was being forced to read, she saw reading more and more as punishment and began to detest it. Lifelong patterns are established in the middle-school and early high-school years, and her parents' strategies were ensuring that Kim would not shape up to be the academically oriented young woman her parents desired.

Mistake number four had to do with Ms. Harley, the English teacher, whose side Janet and Donald took in conversations with Kim on a daily basis. Kim complained about the way Ms. Harley taught English, and she wasn't alone in her feelings. Ms. Harley managed to reduce the most beautiful works of literature to ten short-answer questions on a pop quiz: What town was Heathcliff's mother from in *Wuthering Heights*? What was Jay Gatsby's favorite color? Ms. Harley seemed like a math teacher disguised as an English teacher: Her approach was completely analytical and memory-based, as though simply remembering the plot details meant that the students had understood the books they read. Although it is important for a teacher to be able to assess which students are doing the reading and which aren't, it's also important to consider the depth of understanding students have of the deeper issues in the books they are assigned. Because Ms. Harley focused solely on surface details, the students were encouraged to do the same. Getting an *A* in Ms. Harley's class was guaranteed if a student bought Monarch Notes for each book and memorized all the plot details and characters. As the students caught on, they stopped reading, since actually *reading* meant that they wouldn't have enough time for *memorizing* what they would be tested on.

Ms. Harley was authoritarian as a teacher, discouraging free and open discussion of the books, and encouraging instead careful plot analysis. In this environment, artistic and sensitive students like Kim get the shaft. Their gifts are not valued in the analytical, detail-oriented environment, and their insights into and appreciation of the books are not sought out. The lack of papers and projects in these sorts of classrooms, and the emphasis instead on tests, means that the Kims of the world don't get to show what they know about what they've read. It's not surprising that they get turned off to English class and reading in general.

Kim may have been stuck with Ms. Harley—or maybe not—but Janet and Donald never investigated any options. They supported Ms. Harley, adopting the "teacher is always right" perspective. The funny thing about parents is that they usually go too far one way or the other—their kids' teachers are either always right or always wrong. Some parents blame teachers year in and year out for their children's shortcomings, even though the same observations arise from different teachers in different schools, even in different states! Other parents, like Donald and Janet, tow the party line: "Ms. Harley is your teacher and you must respect her way of doing things. Plot summaries are important: They prove you've read the book. Now go and draw up a plot summary to help you study for the test."

For kids like Kim, this technique simply doesn't work. Kim wants to *experience* the literature she reads. Her past teachers helped her connect with the books they assigned, and this kept Kim reading and loving it. But Ms. Harley couldn't have motivated the Pope to read the Bible. Kim suffered for this inadequacy on the part of her teacher, and her parents only made things worse by always taking Ms. Harley's side and never even acknowledging Kim's unmet needs regarding how best to learn about literature. This situation was pretty ironic, considering that Donald was a university professor of English—you might have thought he'd recognize the shortcomings of Ms. Harley's approach. But Donald was so busy writing his new book of criticism on great works of medieval philosophy that he didn't even notice.

Another losing strategy for Kim, given the dynamics in her family, had to do with her parents' tendency to hold Alison and Ronny up as role models . . . to an almost nauseating degree. Yes, Ronny and Alison were bright, good students who blossomed in the school environment, but Kim didn't need to be reminded of their near-perfect records and academic aspirations every second, particularly when her own successes went largely unrecognized. From Kim's point of view, her achievements were equally significant to those of her older sister (winning second place in the science fair) and her younger brother (getting placed into an advanced reading class). Kim played the flute and piano beautifully, sang well, acted well, and painted wonderfully, but her parents never cared about these accomplishments because they did not involve core academic subjects. Kim already knew about Ronny and Alison's strategies for school success: She didn't need to be reminded every day that her brother and sister studied long hours at the dinner table. It did absolutely no good to rub her nose in their stellar successes; it only caused resentment to develop among the siblings. Interestingly, because Janet was herself a deeply competitive person, she reasoned that competition among her kids would make each of them strive harder. But this approach does not work for children like Kim, who are sensitive and who step to their own drummers. Children like Kim tend to withdraw from competition rather than face it headlong.

A related mistake Kim's parents made was in rarely attending her plays and recitals. True, Janet worked long hours and Donald did his best writing at night, but Kim ended up feeling even more alienated from her family when her parents missed an event. She responded by identifying more with her vocal teacher and the kids in the play, adopting more artistic values and abandoning the academic values her parents represented. This dynamic was being reinforced in Kim's mind so often that she began to feel as if she had been adopted—it just didn't seem like she fit in with the rest of her family.

Another overall poor strategy by Kim's parents was to turn reading into a mandated activity. Reading soon became a dreaded daily chore; something Kim used to love but now reviled. By forcing Kim to read books Ms. Harley chose, her parents participated in Harley's rule of tyranny (at least that's how Kim saw it). Ms. Harley never let the students read what they wanted to. And when Kim brought home a romance novel from the library along with some books on painting and an anthology of great Broadway plays, were her parents excited that she was reading—and not only *reading*, but bringing books home from the library on her own? No way! Furious at her selection of such garbage, they forbade her to read that crap and insisted she pick up *Moby Dick* instead. There's a piece of insight: What fourteen-year-old girl wouldn't relate to the Ahab character and the white-whale imagery? (It was time for these parents to open their eyes.) As Donald remarked, "I'd rather die than see my own flesh and blood poring over a piece of pulp-fiction trash! I certainly hope you didn't let anyone we know see you with that book." This may sound extreme, but Donald was being considered for an endowed chair, and he had to maintain the family's academic image.

Maybe you're feeling a bit sorry for Kim; she certainly was. Fortunately, there were some workable, winning strategies that could turn things around and get Kim excited about reading again. And this was one family that needed a few winning strategies!

In a very real sense, people who have read good literature have lived more than people who cannot or will not read. . . It is not true that we have only one life to live; if we can read, we can live as many more lives and as many kinds of lives as we wish.
—S. I. HAYAKAWA

WINNING STRATEGIES

The single biggest winning strategy for this family has to do with changing counterproductive attitudes. First, there are Janet and Donald's attitudes toward Kim, academic success, and family life. These parents need a reality check: They think they have a monster in their midst, when in reality they have a winner. Sure, she was having a few problems, but she was fourteen and in her first year of high school. Janet and Donald cared a lot about their children, but they often expected too much from them. Case in point was Kim. The solution to Kim's reading problems will depend on her parents' realigning their expectations to be more in keeping with reality. Perhaps they could talk to a few teachers and others parents and get more in touch with what typical fourteen-year-olds are like. Janet and Donald are insulated in their jobs, and they don't meet many other parents of adolescents. It might help for Kim's parents to expose themselves to more kids by attending some school events and making an effort to meet other parents. The reality check provided by this seat-of-the-pants comparison of their daughter with the drug-using indigents in the ninth grade might help them to ease up on her!

The fact is that, like most of us, Kim occasionally made mistakes in how she budgeted her time preparing for school, because her other interests were more compelling than her work on academic subjects. The key word here is *mistake:* Kim was not doing it intentionally, she was slipping up. When Janet confronted Kim accusingly, she sent the message that she believed her daughter was screwing up on purpose just to annoy her. This lawyer-logic doesn't and shouldn't be applied to a fourteen-year-old.

Next, Kim's parents have to readjust their attitude toward academic success. Bright people like Janet and Donald often take for granted the fact that superior academic accomplishments are all that matters in life—you know, the type of people who begin conversations by asking where you went to school, when you're clearly pushing forty. The recognition that Kim doesn't share this value may be painful, but it also could become a broadening experience for the family. Not everyone measures success by reaching the same goalpost, and Kim was waiting in line to join the other team. By softening their attitude somewhat, Donald and Janet would open the door to honest communication with Kim about her own personal values and goals. And this brings us to the third area of attitude adjustment.

Janet and Donald also need to realign their attitudes regarding their family life. Kim was fourteen; in four years she'd be on her own, even if this did mean she was doing pantomime in Central Park for food money. As is typical of many bright and supposedly enlightened parents, Donald and especially Janet ran the household like prison wardens. Their kids were kept on a strict schedule in which "free fun time" was penciled in every other day for one hour. News flash: These were children, not inmates. The parents saw a work ethic and discipline as the roots of success, so they did their best to instill these values in their kids. Alison and Ronny felt loved and appreciated, but this was because they were naturally successful in the areas their parents valued and did just as their parents asked. But Kim was her own person, different from her siblings, and her parents spent an inordinate amount of energy trying to make her comply with their wishes. They acted like they could sculpt the daughter they wanted out of clay. They were mistaken, and Kim railed against the overly intrusive attempts to control her and re-create her in their own image.

With regard to Alison and Ronny, it would be wise for Janet and Donald to remember that when they praise their accomplishments, whether within the family or to outsiders, they should also mention one of Kim's successes. This might seem foreign at first, since Alison and Ronny are academic superstars. But Kim's work is equally impressive in its own way, and Alison and Ronny aren't as musically or artistically talented as Kim (not by a long stretch). It's important in multi-sibling families for each child to feel that her or his individual gifts and talents are recognized and appreciated.

A bit of attitude readjustment would help with the situation at school, too. Had Janet and Donald been open to the possibility that Ms. Harley had a limited approach to teaching English and used many questionable strategies, they might have been able to tactfully suggest a reassignment for Kim based on the fact that Kim loved drama and the other English teacher was also the drama coach (or some other creative reason). Kim told her parents enough examples for them to have picked up on the sorry truth. There are a lot of Ms. Harleys out there, and when kids give specific examples, they're often right. Kim wasn't a liar—her parents could have trusted her and helped her change to another class. Now it was February, but better late than never. Janet and Donald could tactfully discuss with the principal their perception that their daughter was mismatched with her English teacher. Maybe the principal would agree with them and give Kim a new class assignment; maybe he'd be willing to switch her after mid-winter vacation. In any case, even if he wasn't willing to switch Kim, Kim would appreciate that her criticisms were taken seriously by her parents. She would also be grateful to them for taking the time to try to help.

And while on the topic of Ms. Harley, another winning strategy is for Janet to stop intruding herself so into Kim's school life. Contact with teachers is one thing, but Janet was muscling in where she didn't belong, arranging extra assignments and tests for her and getting overly involved in her daughter's entire school experience. Kim was sensitive about her mother's pushy and intrusive nature, and this overinvolvement with school only made it worse. Kim is generally a very good student—she doesn't need a mother who treats her like a delinquent. By taking this tack, Janet encourages and validates Ms. Harley's rigid and overly intrusive style, which does nothing to help with Kim's reading problem.

The best outcome of the needed attitude shifts by Janet and Donald will be a new dynamic between Kim and her folks. Whereas before, her parents would tell her what to do and how to do it and punish her for failing, now they will sit down with Kim and discuss the situation. They will explain that they sense a growing problem with Kim's attitude toward academics and state how they feel about the situation. Then they must listen to Kim and really *hear* her side. Finally, they should ask Kim how the family can solve the problem by working *together*. Kim needs to be heard and validated. She needs to be a part of the solution to her problem. Feeling a part of the solution will make Kim more open to changing her counterproductive behavior patterns for the better, instead of simply reacting against her parents' goals for her life.

A few specific winning strategies to get Kim reading again include encouraging her to read whatever she wants: romance novels, adult novels, books on drama and biographies of actors, books on painting, you name it. (Donald could buy the stuff in a nearby town and wrap it in plain brown paper to avoid being seen with it!) It would be great if Donald could take Kim to the bookstore and have her pick out a few pieces of trash (as Donald would describe it) that she liked. They could also make a trip to the library. It would be tough, but Donald's task would be to stop telling his daughter what to read! He loved medieval philosophy, but for a fourteen-year-old, *The Myth and the Mystic* isn't exactly a page turner. A lot of goodwill would be created if Kim felt that her father didn't despise everything she enjoyed in life.

Janet and Donald could use Kim's birthday and holidays to give her books she would like. Maybe Mr. Wong could provide a few suggestions—perhaps books about theater and singing. Mr. Wong might even be persuaded to begin encouraging his students to read certain books related to their work on the play and in vocal class. Maybe a novel about a great singer or actress could be suggested by Mr. Wong, with a few copies provided to the class for sign-out. If Mr. Wong was willing, he might read to the class a few sections he personally liked to whet kids' appetites and get them interested. The key here is to recruit a likely sympathizer like Mr. Wong to help get the kids in his class to read more. Because it's not a core academic subject, there would be a lot of leniency in what he suggested they read. The reading wouldn't even be required. Because the subject matter would be interesting to the kids and relevant to their real-life experiences in Mr. Wong's class, they would be likely to read the books for fun. Just what the doctor ordered, plus, the other kids would benefit just as much as Kim by being reminded (or learning for the first time) that reading is fun.

At home at night Janet could ask Kim about the romance novel she's reading or the new book on the theater she got from the library. Janet could ask Kim's opinion of the romance novel because someone at work reads them and Janet would like to buy this woman one as a gift. Or Janet could ask Kim's opinion about whether books on painting actually help Kim paint better, and if so, how. The point is that this should be a *discussion* instead of an *interrogation,* a chance for Kim to talk about books in a nonthreatening and nonacademic context. Janet could also ask the school or local librarian to come up with a list of possible books for Kim, and bring a couple home for her. Kim would appreciate the fact that her mother had taken the time from her busy schedule to pick out books for her.

Another way for the family to capitalize on Kim's interests would be to let her plan a family trip for next summer, possibly to a place Kim has always wanted to visit. The goal would be for Kim to write away for and buy materials about several places, and do enough research for the family to decide what they would do in each place and ultimately to make the decision of where to go. If she was motivated enough, Kim might do a thorough background check on two or three places, then present the information to her family for a group decision. Again, this idea capitalizes on Kim's love of travel and desire to see the world. She's too young to be crossing the Australian outback alone, but maybe she can convince her parents that the Grand Canyon's not so bad, and maybe her father can arrange to give a couple of talks at a university in Arizona while he's there, to offset the expense. This family has to remember to link reading to Kim's interests, to stop making reading a chore, to stop requiring that she read, and to stop criticizing what Kim reads. Connecting with Kim as a human being with interests and values of her own and validating her desire to read what she wants to read is the biggest winning strategy of all.

A book is like a garden carried in the pocket.
—*CHINESE PROVERB*

MORALS OF KIM'S STORY

How to Get and Keep Kids Reading

• If you are an academic or someone who loves great literature and reading, accept that your child may not share your values. Let your child read what is interesting to her.

• If you are pressing your child to read more when her grades are good, you may be pushing too hard.

- Don't criticize your child for failing to read if you never praise her for being successful at other activities.

- If your child is artistic, recognize that she may choose to spend all her recreational time on artistic activities. Encourage reading by choosing books related to these activities (books on music, art, theater, etc.).

- If your child's siblings are academically oriented and read a lot, don't rub this in your reluctant reader's face. Don't talk up the siblings' accomplishments while criticizing the reluctant reader.

- Don't try to *force* a sensitive child to read with stringent demands and standards—instead, *encourage* reading with tantalizing materials and freedom to explore them.

- Resist the temptation to plan your child's entire academic future and to announce these plans—it could turn your child off to reading by making her anxious, afraid to fail, and afraid of not measuring up to your expectations.

- Don't respond to occasional lapses in schoolwork in an otherwise good student with harsh punishments—instead, provide assistance in dealing with the cause of the lapse and support in correcting the situation.

- As soon as you begin to sense a problem with reading, sit down and ask your child her view of the situation. Listen to her side and ask her to work with you to solve the problem.

- Don't muscle in and get overly involved with teachers' classroom methods. If your child is a good student who has an occasional lapse, don't talk to her teacher before discussing the situation with your child. Your child will feel violated by you and will see you as banding together with her teacher to punish her. Give the teacher a chance to solve the problem her own way—resist telling the teacher what to do!

• Don't obsess about imperfect performance in a good student. We all make mistakes! Don't catastrophize the situation or you'll teach your child that mistakes are not tolerated, and this can make her feel like a failure.

CHAPTER SIX

AFRAID OF NOT MEASURING UP: CHASE'S STORY

I read Shakespeare and the Bible, and I can shoot dice. That's what I call a liberal education.
—TALLULAH BANKHEAD

When you read a classic, you do not see more in the book than you did before; you see more in you than there was before.
—CLIFTON FADIMAN

Chase fidgeted on the bench as his teammates tried to score a goal against what looked like impossible odds. The hockey team from the school across town had a Canadian kid on the ice this year, and he had obviously grown up pantomiming Wayne Gretzky. "He must have been skating before he could walk! Look at him go!" ten-year-old Chase said to his friend Peter, who sat equally nervously next to him on the bench. The seconds felt like eternities as the clock ticked down. Chase's team was 6 and 1 for the season—soon to be 6 and 2. The coach, Mr. Devon, looked resigned to their demise at the hands of the Canadian assassin. Chase looked down and bit his lip, and just then the buzzer sounded, jolting him to his soul.

Back in the locker room, the boys from the home team had to endure the teasing and badgering of the bruisers from the North End and their Canadian hitman. Chase and Peter took the situation very seriously for fifth graders, walking somberly, towels in hand, to the shower.

"What are we going to tell our fathers?" Chase asked.

"My dad already knows—he was sitting in the second row!" answered Peter.

"Oh. Well my dad is at a meeting or something, but Mom will remind him there was a game and I'll have to explain why we lost."

"Don't worry about it, Chase," Peter said. "It's just our number-one ranking!"

"Thanks a lot, you butthead," Chase shot back, as he lathered up.

Peter and Chase walked back to their lockers feeling as self-assured as lame footmen. After another couple of minutes in the hockey morgue, Peter couldn't stand it anymore, so he changed the subject. He started talking about the new compact disk store at the mall where you could listen to the CDs on a special computer before you bought them. Chase was enthralled. Peter was going to the mall with his mother the next day after school, and he invited Chase along. This was the boys' favorite activity, and on days when they didn't have hockey practice they would get Peter's sister or mother or sometimes Chase's mother to take them to the mall. Then they'd spend two hours going through compact disks and spending their allowance money at the arcade playing video games.

Dressed and ready, gear in hand, Chase and Peter waited in the vestibule with faces like doormen at a funeral parlor. Chase's mother, Victoria, saw her son and pulled up in the Volvo wagon with the heat on high. Chase got in and started apologizing from the moment his aching body hit the seat. He knew his parents, and especially his father, cared about the ranking of the school's sports teams. His father had gone to the same private school when he was a kid, and sports had always been a big thing. Chase's younger sister Catherine played lacrosse, and she was learning tennis and figure skating this year. Now ten and a half, Chase had been playing hockey since he was six. He had also tried his hand at football, squash, and tennis. The school piled on the sports stuff—lots of slogans about team spirit and character building and all that. But tonight the team had lost—*lost*—and moved to number two in the district. Chase was crushed, and for once even Mr. Devon, the coach, had nothing to say.

As the car pulled in the driveway of their house, Chase asked if his father was home yet. His mother replied that he was at a work strategy session and wouldn't be home until ten or so. *Thank God,* Chase thought, dragging his tired flesh upstairs. "Better work on your reading, honey," his mother called up the stairs. "I left a new library book for you on the nightstand. Remember our agreement." Chase rolled his eyes and heaved out a sigh as he walked into his room to find another Dickens book next to his bed. *Who does she think I am?* he wondered. *It's late, I'm exhausted . . . plus, does anyone ever read this stuff?*

Then his sister Catherine ran in and punched Chase in the stomach, showing off her new muscles. "How'd the game go?"

"We sucked!" Chase answered. "Cathy, I'm beat, and I haven't even started my homework. Can you please cut me some slack?"

"Sure, jerkface loser!" Cathy answered, skipping out the door as she sang "loser—loser—loser" to the tune of their school's fight song. "Everyone's a comedian," Chase muttered, as he picked up his math-exercise book and lay down on the bed.

Chase worked through his math exercises, then looked over at the Dickens book. It was *David Copperfield.* Chase knew he had to read some every night, especially if he wanted to earn the money his mother had promised him. She had decided back in September, at the start of fifth grade, that her son had to buckle down and do some serious reading. So she had agreed to pay him extra allowance money of ten dollars per week plus a bonus of twenty dollars for every book he finished. She would quiz him on the books when he said he was done to make sure he hadn't flipped through them without reading them. Part of the agreement was that Vicky would pick out the books she thought Chase should read, either at the bookstore or library or off her and her husband's shelves. Vicky believed that most of what kids read nowadays is garbage, "stuff that should be burned rather than read," and she was determined that her son rise above the crowd and get a decent grounding in literature. Since Chase had virtually no interest in the books his mother thought he should read, she made the deal to pay him for his progress. She reasoned that, in time and with maturity, Chase would learn to enjoy reading the books and move ahead without the financial incentive. Plus, at least for now the tactic got him reading the material he needed to be exposed to.

Chase caught himself drifting off to sleep and shook his head a couple of times. He couldn't remember a thing about the chapter he had been reading. Usually he passed over the words with his eyes, but his mind wandered until eventually he either fell asleep or became so engaged in thinking about something else that he put the book down. Tonight it was the former. The long day at school and the hockey game had seen to that. Chase was exhausted, but he had set his sights on a couple of new compact disks at the mall and wanted the money from his mother to buy them this weekend. Chase was glad his father wasn't home. He hated the third degree he had to endure when one of his teams lost.

Winning at sports wasn't the only type of winning that mattered to Chase's father. Bradley was an equal-opportunity disciplinarian: He was demanding of his son in every area. Chase was expected to play on winning teams, be placed into the brightest classes at school, get high grades, and eventually attend the same elite schools as had his father. When his father came home, Chase would feel his body tensing and his stomach beginning to ache. It seemed like nothing he ever accomplished was good enough for his dad. If he brought home a report card with four As and one B, his father would attack and question him about the "poor grade." Bradley's standards were high, and he fully expected his son to meet them. Fortunately, Brad's career in the banking industry meant frequent travel and late nights at the office. On these occasions Chase would get a reprieve from the third degree and actually get to relax a bit after school.

Finally Chase was ready to give up. It was ten o'clock and he had to get some sleep. He only vaguely remembered what he had read tonight, despite spending almost an hour at the task . . . something about a guy named Ham who drowned . . . Chase didn't really care.

Instead of feeling good about the reading he had done, he felt guilty because he knew he should have spent some time on his school reading assignment for Mr. Stillwell's class tomorrow. But he wasn't interested in what Mr. Stillwell had assigned any more than he was interested in *David Copperfield*, so he figured he might as well go for the cash. Chase leaned over, turned out the light, and fell sound asleep in his sweatsuit just as his father's car pulled in the driveway.

Downstairs, Vicky looked up from her *Gourmet* magazine to greet her husband. Predictably, his first question was, "So how did the team do?" Vicky said they had lost, describing the role of the Canadian kid who was a year older than the others, had been left back a grade because of his family's relocation to the United States, and skated like he was possessed. Brad laughed, shook his head, and poured himself a scotch. "That's no excuse! If Chase and his team only had good defense, the Canadian hotshot wouldn't have been able to make those goals."

"Oh, well, dear; they're only in fifth grade, and it's only a game," Vicky answered, returning to her magazine.

Brad flipped on the news and put his feet up. "I'll give Chase some pointers over the weekend," he said. "How's he doing with his reading? Have you talked to Stillwell lately? Just because it's hockey season doesn't give Chase the right to lighten up on schoolwork!" Brad snapped a few more comments, then settled down to a couple of hours of television and Chivas Regal. Vicky sighed and said she'd call Mr. Stillwell tomorrow.

The next morning Vicky got the kids to school by eight o'clock and thought about stopping to talk to Mr. Stillwell in person. She pondered her decision, rubbing the back of her neck as the various consequences of the likely discussion ran through her mind. Ultimately, she decided to talk to Chase first, knowing that things between her son and his English teacher were already tense enough. She figured that if she approached Mr. Stillwell now, at eight o'clock, Chase might receive an unexpected response when he got to English class at nine. So she went on to the mall to catch the early-bird sale at her favorite clothing store.

Why did Brad always have to be so hard on Chase? she thought as she drove down the highway. He was a good kid, he did his work, he got good grades, and he got along well with other people. Their friends all said they'd love to have a kid like Chase. But Brad just wouldn't lighten up. He acted like Chase was twenty, not ten and a half. Brad expected too much of his son.

Next thing Vicky knew, she was at the exit and her thoughts immediately turned to the off-white wool coat she wanted to buy.

At that very moment, Chase filed into Mr. Stillwell's class behind the sixteen other victims. He felt like a lamb being led to the slaughterhouse. Mr. Stillwell was universally feared by all the kids at school. He was sixty-three and had been teaching English in the same classroom for over thirty-five years. And things hadn't changed much in the way he taught over those years—children had come and gone, *their* children had come and gone, but Mr. Stillwell still taught the old-fashioned way: The way *he* had been taught, of course. Fred Stillwell was like an institution within an institution. He had been employed by the school longer than any of the other teachers or administrators, and his colleagues respected his dedication to teaching and excellence in a time of declining standards in education. Mr. Stillwell was cantankerous and difficult, to be sure, but underneath he was not a cruel person, but rather an extremely demanding teacher who insisted on old-fashioned values and respect from children whose own parents hadn't been taught with such a conservative approach. (Except for Bradley, of course.)

The students sat, mechanically opened their notebooks, and took out their copies of *Lord of the Flies*. Mr. Stillwell looked up and began reading aloud from chapter 2. A girl in the third row snickered, and Mr. Stillwell stopped reading to glare at her. Chase sat fidgeting in the last row, trying to follow along with the story, but his attention wandered. He was worried because he hadn't had the time to read chapter 2 at home. His classmates had read the chapter, and Chase knew it was only a matter of time before Mr. Stillwell called on him and he would look like an idiot. Chase was also worried about what he would tell his father if his English grade didn't go up on his next report card. At the thought, his stomach became tense and he took a deep breath.

Just then the heinous, dreaded event happened: "Chase! Can you illuminate the class please? What do you think Golding was trying to say about human nature?" Mr. Stillwell looked Chase straight in the eye. Chase froze in his seat. "Stand up please, and answer the question, Chase. What was the author trying to say about human nature?"

"I don't know, sir," Chase answered tentatively.

"Take a guess, Chase. What do you think the author was trying to say about human nature?" Just in case Chase (or another classmate) had forgotten the question, Mr. Stillwell repeated it a fourth time. Chase stood mum, feeling like an idiot, overwhelmed with self-doubt and anxiety. Mr. Stillwell was relentless. "Chase.

Do you hear me, young man? What was Golding trying to say about human nature?" By now several classmates were snickering, and Chase's best friend Peter was giving him a look of pure agony.

"Mr. Stillwell, sir, I'm sorry, but I don't know the answer to the question," Chase said softly.

"Speak up, young man!" Mr. Stillwell glared and stood up to his full intimidating height of six feet and three inches.

"I'm sorry, Mr. Stillwell, sir," Chase projected, "but I do not know the answer."

"Very well, then, sit down, and see me after class."

Chase sat down, his face and ears burning, his stomach queasy.

Chase spent the next thirty minutes feeling like an inmate on death row. He feared the worst, and in this case his fear was justified. Mr. Stillwell had spoken to him repeatedly about his poor performance in English class. Mr. Stillwell had also called his mother several times over the year. This teacher was like a cur with a bone. Once he got his mind fixated on a student, he was relentless. Mr. Stillwell was determined to whip Chase into shape, whatever it took to accomplish this feat with a ten-year-old. As the bell rang, Chase stood up and approached Mr. Stillwell's desk with the look of a prison camp survivor. Mr. Stillwell saw the pained look on Chase's face, but he was determined.

"Chase! I take it you did not complete your reading assignment. Do you have an excuse—and please do not even consider using the hockey game last night as a reason for shortchanging an academic assignment!" Chase's stomach went from queasy to downright sick. Mr. Stillwell continued, "You give me no other choice, young man. I believe it is time for a conference with both of your parents. We've got to set up a system that works; this problem is not being solved on its own. I will call your mother after lunch. Do you have anything to say in your defense before I do?"

Chase's mind went blank. All he could think about was the humiliation he had endured in front of the class, and the sure punishment he would endure at home once Mr. Stillwell called his mother—and worse, met with both his parents! "No, sir," Chase answered.

"You are excused," Mr. Stillwell said, returning to his desk.

Chase slouched out the door, already late to his next class. Mr. Stillwell sat down, feeling disappointed about the interaction. In truth he liked Chase and did not enjoy being tough on him. But he believed his approach was the best thing for the boy, the principled way to handle the situation. Mr. Stillwell thought Chase was clearly one of the brightest children in the fifth grade, and he worried about the boy's lack of concentration and focus. It was one thing when Chase was hyperactive in the second grade; but this was fifth grade, the academic demands were getting more rigorous, and success in school increasingly meant concentrating and carrying out assignments at home. Although he did not relish the thought of being responsible for Chase's being punished, Mr. Stillwell believed that involving Chase's parents was the only option to help the boy at this point.

The telephone conversation did not go well. When she heard that Chase was failing to read his English assignments, Vicky became so agitated that she began ranting at Mr. Stillwell. "But what are we going to do about it? He's always been a child with lots of energy. The sports events are important to him and his father.

I send him to his room every day for homework time and reading time. I help him every time he asks. Our family reads all the time, but Chase has never shared our pleasure in books. Even his sister reads more than he does, and she's nine! Chase can hardly sit still to read, unless it's because he's so tired and burned out from his day that he has no more energy. That's when he can get through a book, but afterward it's like he hasn't even looked at it—he doesn't remember anything!"

Mr. Stillwell thought for a minute, then answered, "I understand that you have tried to help your son. I'm not sure what the answer is; all I know is that the problem is serious and becoming more so. Chase can't concentrate on his homework, and he's beginning to fall behind. I suggest you discuss the situation with your husband, and then the three of us can meet to work out some sort of plan."

Vicky thanked Mr. Stillwell and hung up. She was terribly upset at the thought of her child being a failure in school—she would never have believed it possible! It was like a cruel joke, like having a child born with a birth defect. This type of horrible thing happened to other families: Her children were as perfect as kids could be, and they had always been well mannered, successful, and well liked by others. Until now, that is. Vicky simply didn't know how to deal with failure like this in a child; she had absolutely no experience with it.

That night, Bradley had the opposite reaction: He became infuriated at the thought of his genetic offspring doing so poorly in a core subject. He knew it was just laziness and lack of hard work. In fact, Mr. Stillwell was only saying something that Brad had suspected for a while—that his son was slacking off and failing to meet his responsibilities. "He'll never get into a decent prep school at this rate! Why can't he be more like Cathy?" Brad snapped at his wife. At this remark, Vicky began to cry and went upstairs to their bedroom. Brad vowed to crack down on Chase and make sure he was spending adequate time on his reading assignments. He went upstairs to have a discussion with his son, but found him sound asleep in bed, his copy of *David Copperfield* still open next to his pillow.

There are two motives for reading a book: one, that you enjoy it; the other, that you can boast about it.
—BERTRAND RUSSELL

A classic is something that everybody wants to have read and nobody wants to read.
—MARK TWAIN

THE PROBLEM

Chase is a young man under intense pressure. At ten and a half, he feels disappointing to *someone* just about every day: his coach, Mr. Stillwell, and, most often, his father. Bradley has high expectations for his son and feels justified in relentlessly maintaining these expectations. "The real world is demanding and unforgiving, and the sooner Chase learns this fact of life, the better," he can be heard repeating, day in and day out. Bradley grew up in a traditional New England family overbrimming with work ethic. His values are hardwired into his skull; it never occurs to him to ask whether some of his beliefs may be out of sync with what's best for his son. Bradley reasons that his values got him where he is today—to a high-paying position with a prestigious financial management group, living in a huge house in a ritzy suburb, with a beautiful and artistic wife and two good-looking children. The family even has the requisite chocolate Labrador retriever. Brad is so proud of his accomplishments that he instinctively wants his son to be created from exactly the same mold. But the trouble is that, like many fathers in similar situations, Bradley doesn't really remember what it was like to be ten years old. He's thinking of his son as a small version of himself, as an adult, when Chase is actually a kid in fifth grade.

Bradley is rarely around. His travel and work schedule take almost all his waking time. Chase never gets a chance to shoot the breeze with his father, to talk about the types of things on a ten-year-old's mind, to get to know his father as a human being. To Chase, Bradley is half mythical superhero and half monster. He does everything right, he's financially successful and talented, and Chase admires him for his many accomplishments and of course because Brad is his dad. Bradley doesn't have much time for his son; when things are going well—the team is winning and the grades are high—Bradley has little more than passing conversations with his son for weeks. But as soon as Chase performs less than perfectly in some life domain, his father is all over him like a cheap polyester suit. Suddenly, Brad has the time to ask what went wrong in the hockey game or why Chase got a B-minus on a book report. Brad sees it as his duty to get involved when his son is slipping, but he never takes the time to praise Chase when the kid is doing well. No wonder Chase gets a stomachache when he hears his father pull in the driveway at night.

Then there's Victoria, who's trying to be a supportive mother. Vicky has involved herself heavily with her son's reading problem, trying everything she can think of to help. Vicky is high strung and sensitive, and she comes unglued at the thought of her son performing less than perfectly at anything. Her life consists of taking care of her two children, decorating and redecorating their large home, fund-raising for the school, working on community action groups, and, when she has time, working on her own art and cooking projects. Vicky's relationship with her husband is somewhat distant and often strained. They have little in common these days except the children, and Vicky has invested a good portion of her self-esteem in her kids. When Chase or Catherine fails at something, Vicky takes it personally. And Bradley doesn't help: His perspective is that Vicky has little else to do except raise the children, so she should be handling the problems that come up without involving him. Bradley is as demanding of Vicky as he is of everyone else.

Chase loves his mother more than anyone in the world; she's the one who's there for him, driving him to hockey games, sitting in the bleachers, sewing his team insignia on his sweatshirt. Chase would adore it if she would spend some time helping him with the homework subjects that trouble him, and especially with his book reports and compositions for Mr. Stillwell's class. But Vicky is uncomfortable getting this involved in her son's school life: Driving him around and packing lunches and snacks is one thing, but Chase's homework is something she doesn't know much about. Plus, this is why the family spends a fortune on private school: so that parents don't have to do the teachers' jobs at home. Bradley keeps saying that Chase's school is one of the best in the country, so Vicky figures there's not much she can do to improve on the education her son is getting there.

Let's not forget Mr. Stillwell; he's certainly part of the problem, too. He's not the ogre the children imagine, but he is a difficult teacher for a boy who's under extreme evaluation pressure and who suffers from performance anxiety. When Chase fidgets and his attention wanders, Mr. Stillwell clamps down like a python. Then Chase becomes more nervous and insecure, and his attention gets more unfocused, and his reading performance suffers further. Then Chase feels even worse about himself, and he worries that his father will find out, and Mr. Stillwell humiliates him in front of the class, and Chase performs even worse and winds up caring about nothing except going to the mall and listening to compact disks by some band with a name people would be excommunicated for repeating in church. Although Mr. Stillwell thinks old-fashioned discipline is the way to whip kids into shape, he's missing the point with Chase. All that's happening is that the kid is being crushed into pulp. Chase no longer believes he can read and perform at the level of the other kids in the class. In truth, Mr. Stillwell thinks highly of Chase's ability, but Chase himself believes he is incompetent at reading.

Unexpectedly, perhaps, Chase's friends contribute in their own way to his problem with reading. His best friend Peter is hardly an academic superstar, and his other friends tend to be members of the sports teams Chase plays on. Peter's favorite activity in life is "getting malled" (literally, going to the shopping mall). Chase's other friends have similar uncerebral interests. Every time Chase's or Peter's mother takes the kids to the mall from 3:00 to 6:00 P.M. and lets them run loose with their allowance money like pack animals released from bondage, these parents are endorsing the mind-numbing behavior of listening to fifty compact disks and spending ten bucks at the arcade on video games. There's not much to recommend about the mall, even for adults. For ten-year-olds it's a disaster. By the time Chase gets home, he's so wired on junk food and candy and his "mall high" that sitting down to read books for Mr. Stillwell is about as likely as Mother Theresa robbing a bank.

So what happened when Mr. Stillwell became concerned enough to call a conference with Chase's parents? Victoria was shaken to the core, Bradley was pissed off, and Chase was terrified. This family tried every losing strategy in the book to make this kid read. If they had kept going in this manner, eventually Chase's prospects for later schooling and career life would have gone supernova. We can all learn a lesson or two from this family's experience.

Some read to think—these are rare; some to write, these are common; and some read to talk, and these form the great majority.
—CHARLES CALEB COLTON

LOSING STRATEGIES

On a global level, the first and biggest losing strategy was engineered by Chase's father. Bradley was convinced that the "no news is good news" approach was the best way to handle interactions with his son. When Bradley was pleased with Chase's progress, he didn't have anything to do with the boy. He reasoned that there was no point in bothering Chase when he was performing well: "If it ain't broke, don't fix it." When something went wrong, though, Brad found out about it faster than a fly on the wall and practically announced the shortcoming to the Associated Press. Suddenly, Chase was the center of attention, and his father wanted to know how much time he had spent reading *Lord of the Flies* every day after school, and how much effort he had put into his composition about the book. Bradley would make it a point to have a great deal of contact with Chase when he perceived that Chase needed the support. From a father's point of view, he was simply making time for his son when his son needed it. But from Chase's point of view, the relationship with his father was not at all what his father imagined.

Chase felt insignificant in his dad's eyes most of the time. No matter how well he did on a math test, or how well he skated in a big game, Bradley was nowhere to be seen. But if Chase missed a key goal his father came out of the woodwork like a Zamboni on overdrive. From Chase's point of view, Bradley didn't care much for him as a person: His interests, his aspirations, his disagreements with friends, and the girls he had crushes on didn't warrant a neuron in his father's brain. All his father cared about was punishing him when he was down, exposing his shortcomings to the world, and lecturing him about the "good old days." The strategy of benign neglect when things were good coupled with "tough love" when things weren't so good made Chase feel insignificant to his father and insecure.

Although his father meant to encourage Chase to perform by cracking down when the boy slipped up, his actions had the opposite effect: When Bradley cracked down, Chase cracked inside, began to doubt himself, and felt like a failure. Instead of reading more and getting involved in his work for Mr. Stillwell's class, Chase would get so unnerved and paralyzed with fear at his self-perceived incompetence that he would withdraw into a shell and stop even trying to succeed. The lesson of Bradley's losing strategy is simple: You cannot be a part-time parent who's only around when your kid screws up. Chase was reading well for a time back in October, and Mr. Stillwell was happy; so happy, in fact, that he gave Chase an *A* for the marking period. But Bradley never even commented to his son that this was a terrific accomplishment for a boy who sometimes had trouble reading and concentrating. Chase didn't get the positive reinforcement he desperately needed from the person he looked up to. Without this well-deserved positive feedback, his self-image suffered and his confidence dipped, and so did his reading performance.

Chase's mother had mustered her own brand of losing strategies. Her tack was to try to get Chase to read the stuff *she* thought he should be reading—the classics, children's poetry, and other books lauded throughout the ages. She would have tried forcing Chase to read the Bible, but it wasn't as high on her priority list as T. S. Eliot poems and Dickens novels. This isn't to say that some children wouldn't have reacted very positively to the choice of *David Copperfield*. But the emotional climate Chase was living in did not favor the love of reading in general—and especially a time-honored but challenging classic (challenging, at least, for most boys Chase's age). Victoria's approach was to pick the books *she* wanted to be able to tell *the other mothers* her son was reading. She'd either buy copies at the bookstore or get them from the library. Then, she'd bribe Chase to read them. Of course, she didn't see it this way; in her view, she was providing necessary encouragement and inducement to her son to engage in meaningful reading. He wanted compact disks at the mall; she knew this meant money. So she used her son's desire for more spending money to get him to read.

What's wrong with this scenario? A lot. First, Vicky was foisting on her son her own ideas of what is worth reading. Maybe some kids would enjoy reading Dickens, but Chase was not one of them. This kid was into sports big-time. But Vicky wouldn't have dreamed of giving him books that focused on topics he liked—she wanted her son to be grounded in the classics. To Chase, the books his mother made him read could cure insomnia. Why did he read them? First, because Vicky coerced him by being distant and detached when he didn't read them. Since his father was emotionally unavailable (and Chase and his sister did not get along well), Chase relied on his mother as his main support structure. He could not bear to be distant from her; her cold-shoulder treatment gave him a stomachache. So he read to please her, or at least he went through the motions of reading.

The second reason why Chase read the books was obvious: for the money. (Perhaps the twenty dollars per book Vicky paid would have induced many of us to slog through some of those weighty tomes.) This was a lot of money to a ten-year-old. And this is the second big reason why Vicky's approach constituted a losing strategy: Parents should not bribe children to read with money on a regular basis, as Vicky was doing. The joy of reading is something a child must feel for himself—he must feel it *inside,* as the pleasure of learning something new or laughing at a funny sentence envelops him. Loving books starts when a kid picks up a book and has fun reading it because it tells him something valuable, interesting, or new to him.

The trouble with bribing kids to read is that all they think about is the money: Particularly if what they're asked to read is uninteresting to them, they often zone out and just follow the words without getting lost in the experience and learning to *love* reading. The money keeps entering their mind . . . what they're going to buy with it, how much they've earned, how soon they'll be able to spend it, and so on. The message from the parents is clear: Reading is a punishment, something without intrinsic joy or reward. One thing it is *not* is fun! If it was fun, the kid wouldn't be offered a bribe to do it. It's obvious that reading is a chore, a daily drudgery to be endured for the cash. The child gets this message loud and clear. Most of us would, and Chase certainly did.

Other losing strategies on Vicky's part included sending Chase to his room alone to read every day. To Chase, this felt like he was serving time. In truth, Vicky wanted to talk to her friends on the phone or work on a new recipe without being interrupted by her son. She reasoned that Chase required quiet time to soak up the material. This sounds like an excuse to me, as it did to Chase. Chase needed help with his reading, and his mother could have been a great resource if she had been willing to take the time to sit with him and go over some of the material. Instead, he was banished to read alone. When he had questions, no one was there to ask. He'd get confused and skip over something, lose the flow of the plot, and stop even trying to follow what was going on. Plus, if Vicky didn't think the books were worth her time, why should Chase?

Another reason why sending Chase off to read alone was a losing strategy was that it meant Vicky had no idea how much time Chase was spending on school reading compared to the extra reading she was paying him to do. In fact, Chase was shortchanging his required school reading to garner the cash. Had Vicky checked up on him, she would have been able to insist that he finish his school reading before beginning the books she had bought for him. But since she adopted the "out of sight, out of mind" approach, she was not aware of the problem.

Vicky was also a culprit in the "malls as entertainment," "video games as entertainment," and "shopping as entertainment" crime. It should be a jailable offense to teach children that spending time in a mall or video arcade is an acceptable thing to do after school. By driving her son to the mall, or by letting him tag along with his friend Peter, Vicky was reinforcing the anti-intellectual values so prevalent in our society. The funny thing is, Vicky prided herself on her vast education and knowledge. Bradley was no less impressed with his educational credentials. But they had tacitly allowed their son to develop a love for commercialism and kitsch instead of following in his bright and talented parents' footsteps. These folks figured that policing their son's performance in school and bribing him to read *Moby Dick* could substitute for real time spent working with him on reading and school projects. They were sadly wrong. The bottom line is that it is far more important *what parents do* than *who parents are:* In other words, less-educated parents who read and work with their children will raise brighter, more successful, and more motivated kids than will highly educated parents who are detached from their children's intellectual development. (This is not just my opinion—major research projects have borne out this fact.)

Another losing strategy was this family's tendency to applaud baby sister Catherine's precocious reading skills as though she were an eight-year-old Olympic medalist. Not to take anything away from Catherine—she was shockingly bright and she deserved praise. That both parents fawned all over her while ostracizing and reprimanding Chase frequently about his reading only made him feel worse. Catherine was a girl, which made a big difference to Bradley. In fact, she was "Daddy's little girl." Brad could be more emotional and sensitive with Catherine because he felt it more appropriate than with his son, a young man. Vicky was also somewhat saccharine with Catherine, the little angel of the family. It's tough when parents have one child with a reading problem and another child who is an academic superstar, or, at least as in Catherine's case, a budding superstar. For Chase, it was tough to compete with Catherine and all that love and attention she received. As a result of feeling that his sister was taking to books and reading faster than he had, Chase only identified further with sports and less-academic pursuits. And his perception that his sister was somehow more pleasing to his father didn't help, either.

This leads us to another strategy that was a real loser with Chase. All the pressure to excel was a heavy cross to bear at his age. His parents piled it on: talking about the school sports teams and how Chase had to do his part to keep the school winning; about how Catherine was looking up to Chase; about how Aunt Ruthy, who had never had any children of her own, was looking to

Chase to fulfill the dreams she would have had for her own son; about how Bradley had been high scorer in nearly every hockey game when he was twelve; about how Chase was going to have to excel if he wanted to get into a good prep school and later a good college; it went on and on. Pressure helps some children who are lazy to strap up and get going. Chase was far from lazy: He worked his butt off, and he was exhausted. The pressure made him tense and nervous. When he didn't measure up he felt like a loser. Plus, he was developing early signs of a peptic ulcer.

Mr. Stillwell also tried some losing strategies—and some winning ones, too, but those were torpedoed by Chase's parents. His efforts were sincere, though often misguided. Like Vicky and Bradley, the teacher layered on the pressure and was skimpy on praise and generous on criticism. His ideas for getting Chase to read often entailed getting Chase's parents involved, as though this would solve the problem in short order. Mr. Stillwell had plenty of clues about Chase's parents and home life: Had he been more open-minded, it might have occurred to him to work with Chase directly instead of throwing another log on the fire. Mr. Stillwell's cracking down hard and threatening Chase with tangible punishments (such as being benched from the hockey team for a week if his book report was late) only made the problem worse. Mr. Stillwell was behaving too much like Chase's father.

Speaking of Mr. Stillwell, what happened in the meeting with Vicky and Brad? Not surprisingly, the folks decided wholeheartedly to implement Mr. Stillwell's ideas for helping Chase. The trouble was that the way they implemented the ideas was not appropriate for *their* son. First, Stillwell suggested that the parents curtail

Chase's involvement in sports for the time being. Brad and Vicky spoke to the coach and arranged to have Chase benched without even discussing the situation with Chase beforehand. This only made Chase less self-confident and more neurotic: Now, in addition to looking like a loser in his family's eyes, he looked like an even bigger nerd and loser in his friends' eyes. For a kid who was lazy and deliberately shirking responsibilities, benching may have been a good strategy to motivate him to work harder. But for Chase, who was unconfident and overwhelmed, the surprise benching humiliated him before his friends and his father and made the problem worse.

Second, Stillwell suggested that Chase's parents apply more at-home reading pressure, forcing Chase to spend more time alone with his books without distractions (telephone, television, etc.). It seems Mr. Stillwell thought Chase spent his after-school time lolling around eating junk food in front of the tube. But in truth Chase already spent quite a bit of time alone in his room, and more time alone was not the answer.

Third, Stillwell suggested that Chase's school reading and projects be prioritized over trips to the mall, visits with friends, and even the reading Vicky was choosing for her son. Hallelujah! Now here were a few good suggestions, but the catch is that the parents wouldn't take any of them: Vicky liked going to the mall, and she liked the free time she had when Chase was visiting friends. She didn't want to sit at home every day with Chase while he did homework. Vicky also thought that the books she required Chase to read were important, and that he should be expected to go through those books after finishing his schoolwork. But we already know that there was one big difference between the books Stillwell assigned and the books Vicky assigned (and it wasn't their interest level to a ten-year-old, which was absolute zero on both accounts). I'm talking about the greenbacks, of course. Chase let his schoolwork and Stillwell's books slide because he wanted the cash his mother paid him for reading the books she chose. So even the good ideas Stillwell offered were a bust, because Chase's parents didn't follow them.

All this said, it is clear that Chase's situation was depressing. He had everything going for him, and nothing going for him, all at the same time. He was smart, athletic, good-looking, and wealthy, but at ten years old he was depressed and neurotic about his reading problem. What could his family do to help?

Books, books, books. It was not that I read so much. I read and reread the same ones. But all of them were necessary to me. Their presence, their smell, the letters of their titles, and the texture of their leather bindings.
—COLETTE

WINNING STRATEGIES

With a few winning strategies this family could help Chase capitalize on his natural talent, intelligence, and tendency to work hard at things that mattered to him. The first and most important of these is a change in perspective on the part of Bradley and Victoria: These parents have to stop putting so much intense pressure on their ten-year-old son. Pushing so hard all the time to make a child perform is hard and exhausting work, and Chase is the most tired one of all. Coupled with this family's high-pressure approach is a pervasive focus on

198 / WENDY M. WILLIAMS, PH.D.

extrinsic goals, incentives, and rewards. This type of focus is often damaging to children; some of the damage is immediately obvious, but other very real damage may go unrecognized until the consequences affect the child years in the future. There has been a wealth of research on the topic of extrinsic versus intrinsic motivation and their relative effects on children's development and performance. How can this research help in choosing winning strategies for Chase?

Consider Chase's situation. His family was wrapped up in appearances and the tangible and material advantages of life. Chase was surrounded by expensive possessions in a beautiful home. *Owning* was as important to this family as *doing*—often more so. The goals of life were to get the best education to secure the best job to earn the most money to buy the biggest house . . . you get the picture. Not much was said about enjoying life or having meaningful experiences. What was important was succeeding in the eyes of the world. Unfortunately, this is a very typical picture in our society. Families who emphasize extrinsic values often pay their children for getting high grades and to induce them to read or do other school tasks. It's natural, because the parents believe that money is the biggest motivator around. Their children want special clothes or music or extra pizza money, and so the parents reason that bribing them is just encapsulating the later lessons of adult life—when we all, presumably, work for a paycheck. Parents with an extrinsic-goal orientation also often place substantial emphasis on grades and societally valued evidence of accomplishment, like scoring high in a hockey game. Again, the key is hard and tangible evidence—external evidence—of success. Wealthy and poor families alike can get caught up in this extrinsic-motivation trap: The key is that possessions and appearances take on a greater importance than meaningful accomplishments and feelings of self-worth and true happiness.

Now consider the opposite picture: that of a family oriented to *intrinsic* motivation and reward. The members of this type of family may live in a lovely home, but unless they inherited it, it probably won't be grand. They may drive cars that are paid for and that are a few years old. Appearances won't matter as much to these people—they tend to be more keyed in to what they believe is right and what they enjoy deep down inside, rather than what their neighbors, friends, or extended family might think. For example, sometimes adults in more intrinsically oriented families will take lower-paying jobs because they believe in the cause or the company. And when it comes to their children, these parents tend to stress learning and loving to learn rather than "getting good grades and scoring goals at any cost." These parents will be concerned that their children benefit from the experience of attending school. They will want their children to earn high grades, but they will care more about their children learning to *internalize* the love of learning. Again, intrinsically motivated parents may be rich or poor. The key is that their lives more often stress inner happiness and personally defined goals rather than societally defined ones.

Intrinsically motivated parents will also realize that they must work with and support their children to develop the love of reading, and they will read to their children from an early age and teach them that books are a wonderful thing. Instead of bribing their kids to read and sending them off to their rooms to log their hours and earn their money, parents with an intrinsic-reward orientation will communicate the joy of reading through their example and by working with their kids.

The net result is that children brought up in an *extrinsically* focused environment will be pushed by their parents and teachers and lured by possessions and other material rewards to learn. They may learn and they may work hard, but their goal will be to get something tangible for their effort. Children brought up in a more *intrinsically* focused environment will tend more to experience the internal joy of learning and reading. They will become self-motivated. These kids will pick up books and do homework because they feel the positive effects inside. Of course, in practice it is not an "all or nothing" thing: Children tend to grow up in mixed environments. But the point is that a more intrinsic, rather than extrinsic, focus is advantageous for children.

In Chase's case, a more intrinsic goal-and-reward orientation was desperately needed. Chase's self-esteem was tied up in whether he scored the most points and won the game, and whether his grades were all *As*, and whether his mother was talking to him or being distant because he hadn't read the latest classic she'd assigned. These issues pervaded his life. Chase never skated because he loved it—he skated because his father had skated. Chase never read something because he was interested in it—he read what his teacher and mother made him read to earn grades, money, and approval. In fact, Chase's whole life was spent pursuing external rewards. His parents had set up their lives in basically this way, and as Chase was growing up he was adopting these values without realizing it, as is often the case with children.

To provide Chase with a different goal structure, the

family has to lower the pressure and shift the focus. Chase needs to feel that reading is something he does for enjoyment, at least sometimes. He needs to feel that all that matters is that he skate his best. Maybe he doesn't want to read the classics; that's fine. Maybe he doesn't want to skate, either—no one ever asked, it was just assumed he would take after his father. Chase's environment has to be redefined to focus on the love of doing and learning for their own sake. If the folks lighten up and let Chase read what he wants and stop being so demanding, this will happen.

So the first specific, concrete winning strategy is for Chase's parents to change the focus of his environment in small ways. By realizing that Chase is never going to make it under the current arrangement, they may gain the self-awareness and motivation to make the necessary changes. First, the daily conversation must be steered away from goals scored, grades earned, and chapters completed. If Chase's father could make it a point to ask him every day about one or two things having to do with what Chase got out of an experience, rather than what he concretely accomplished, the focus would start to be redefined. Brad could ask, "What do you think of the book? Do you like it?" or "How did you enjoy the game?" or "What would you like to be reading if you had a choice?" Chase might be shocked at first, but gradually he would see that his father cares about more than just winning and grades.

Another winning strategy is for Chase's parents actively to encourage him to read anything and everything he likes—comic books, kid's books, sports magazines, anything, as long as it's reading. This way Chase will learn that at least some reading is fun. He'll also learn that his parents care about what he likes.

Maybe Vicky could take Chase to a bookstore and help him find the young adult sport section. This would be far healthier than abandoning him with ten bucks in the video arcade with his friends while she looks at new stemware. Brad could pick up sports magazines or other reading material Chase might like and give it to him at the end of the day. This would make a statement that he wasn't too busy to spend the time to pick something up for his son.

And speaking of Brad, a real winning strategy is for him to spend more time with his son, time that has nothing to do with pressure or tangible rewards for performance. It would be nice for Chase to be able to talk with his father about the fight he just had with his best friend and to get some advice about how to handle his feelings. Maybe Brad could go bike riding with Chase (or anything that doesn't involve winning, losing, and keeping score), and afterward take him to a bookstore and browse. Little efforts like this will help Chase relax and learn that life is fun, as it should be for a ten-year-old. Plus, the peptic ulcer pains will go away once Chase stops obsessing about achievement and winning all the time.

Vicky's winning strategy must be to stop sending Chase off like a leper to read alone in his room. She should make time to work with her son, even if it means waiting a day to try a new recipe. Chase needs to feel that his mother is involved and that she cares. Especially if she stops bribing him to read books he hates, Chase will come to see his mother as more of an ally in learning. This doesn't mean Chase should never be given a financial gift when he's done something good— occasional recognition of accomplishment with money is okay as long as it doesn't become a "fee for service" arrangement.

And both parents must stop favoritizing their little angel Catherine. Constantly talking up Catherine's accomplishments is hurtful to their sensitive son when they never mention any of his. If the parents say something wonderful about Catherine, they should make it a point to say something wonderful about Chase: He has his own gifts, though they may be different from Catherine's. He must feel that his gifts are valuable to himself and to his parents. If Catherine is openly mean and nasty to Chase, as she is wont to be, the parents could point out some less-than-perfect attribute of hers and firmly explain that her meanness must stop (and they must be serious about it). Catherine is often a brat, and being more disciplined with her is a winning strategy for the whole family.

In general, the winning outlook is to reward Chase for *effort* rather than for concrete accomplishment. This will help Chase focus on effort instead of outcome, and he will feel less twisted into a knot inside when he fails. Lazier kids may need a focus on accomplishment, but Chase was OD-ing on this orientation. By focusing on effort, and praising effort, the parents will help Chase relax. Then his natural ability will function more effectively. He'll start performing better and feeling better about himself. He'll think, *What's important is to try* rather than *What's important is to win*. This is the change in focus that will make all the difference.

What about Mr. Stillwell? He had a few good suggestions, but the parents ignored them. Mr. Stillwell was right to suggest that Chase's athletic involvements be scaled down a *bit*—but he was wrong to say that Chase should be benched 100 percent with no forewarning or discussion. The kid needs time to sit and learn to love reading, and he can't do it at eight o'clock at night, because by then he's too tired. Bradley should stop obsessing about Chase's following in his footsteps. Bradley was a great skater; this doesn't mean Chase has to be. It would be better for Chase to learn to love books and school projects than to be a high scorer. But for this to happen, Bradley has to lighten up and start living in the present. This is Chase's life, and he should be allowed to develop into his own person with his own hobbies and interests. Mr. Stillwell also suggested that Vicky stop pushing Chase to read the extra stuff she thought her culture-impoverished son needed. Stillwell was right. This was too much pressure for a kid. There's plenty of time later for Dickens and Eliot. So, some of Mr. Stillwell's insights were winning ones.

But Stillwell was part of the problem, too. To turn the interaction between Chase and Stillwell around, Vicky and Bradley should sit down and have an honest talk with him. They should let this dedicated but old-fashioned teacher know how much they value his degree of commitment and caring for their son. They could then suggest that the family and Mr. Stillwell work together to support Chase's reading progress. Perhaps Mr. Stillwell would respond positively to the suggestion that, despite the fact that many kids profit from a tough approach, Chase needs somewhat less toughness and somewhat more positive reinforcement. Stillwell might see that his approach has been less than perfect and become a part of the solution. If he doesn't respond positively, Vicky and Brad could do their best to help their son at home and counteract Stillwell's negative influences. They could explain to Chase that Stillwell cares, even though he has an odd way of showing it at times. Explaining to Chase how things look from Stillwell's perspective isn't a bad idea, either. Chase is smart enough to know that Stillwell grew up in a different era—a blind person could see this straight off. Maybe if Chase had more insight into Stillwell, he could work more productively with him. Plus, just by getting his grades up, which will happen naturally when the pressure is eased, a lot of the tension between Chase and Mr. Stillwell will be dissipated.

The overall change from emphasizing *extrinsic* motivators, goals, rewards, and winning performance to emphasizing *intrinsic* motivators, goals, rewards, and effort will help solve Chase's reading problems and his other school and outside-of-school problems, too. Chase often has trouble concentrating because his life is so fragmented and there are so many demands on his time. He will concentrate better and focus more effectively when his schedule is relaxed and his time more his own. And he will overcome his reading problems by being given material to read that he likes and by having his parents lighten up and let him be ten years old, at least for the time being.

If we encounter a man of rare intellect, we should ask him what books he reads.
—RALPH WALDO EMERSON

MORALS OF CHASE'S STORY

How to Get and Keep Kids Reading

• Stop forcing on your child your own ideas and values about what he should be reading. The key word here is *force*. Unless you can convey your values in a positive way with an enthusiasm that is contagious, you will achieve the opposite of your goal: abhorrence of your suggestions. A general rule of thumb is that as long as school reading is completed, let your child read whatever he wants—you want him to discover that reading is fun and that it provides information valuable *to him*.

• Don't attack your child's failures and forget to praise other successes. Instead, discuss reading problems within the context of what your child is good at—showing that reading skills can be acquired just like these other skills were.

• Don't regularly pay kids to read! It keeps them from developing intrinsic motivation (the desire to read because it's fun).

• Help your child understand the behavior of difficult teachers by explaining the situation from the teachers' point of view, and by listening to and validating your child's perceptions of the situation.

• Tell your child often that he is bright and capable. Mention past reading successes and stress that they can be repeated.

• Don't become emotional about your child's reading problem—don't panic! Many children have reading problems at some point. With help, your child can solve the problem and suffer no permanent effects. Never catastrophize the problems in front of your child!

• Don't just talk to your child about reading when there's a problem. Interact on a daily basis about everything that matters to your child, including reading.

• Don't openly applaud the academic or reading accomplishments of supersiblings or friends while implying criticism of your reluctant reader. Stress each child's gifts and the value of effort in attaining them.

- Encourage your child to associate with friends and peers who read often and enjoy books. Limit time spent at malls, stores, etc. (unless they are bookstores!).

- Don't pressure your child to follow in your own reading-oriented footsteps—don't hold yourself up as a paragon of reading. Offer help and encouragement instead of a lecture about your own successes.

- Don't use reading as a punishment or you'll teach kids that reading is a chore to be dreaded.

- Know your child: Some kids are helped by pressure, while others crumble. Look honestly at whether pressure helps or hinders your child's performance, and respond appropriately. More pressure doesn't necessarily mean better performance!

- Consider meeting with difficult teachers for an open talk about your child's problem. Perhaps you'll get some new insights about helping your child if you give these teachers a chance. Or maybe you'll confirm for yourself that they truly are the dipsticks your child says they are!

- If your child has performance anxiety, ask him about how he feels and what he likes and dislikes rather than about the outcomes of events: "How did you feel about the test?" and "What did you like about the game?" rather than "What was your grade?" and "Did you win?"

75 QUICK WAYS TO GET AND KEEP KIDS READING

I cannot live without books.
—THOMAS JEFFERSON

- Have fun with reading: Link reading with pleasure in kids' minds.
- Read aloud to children starting when they're young.
- Have reading materials around where kids will see them.
- Be seen reading and enjoying it—quoting, laughing, learning, sharing, etc.
- Take kids to the library often and show them how to use its resources.
- Show that you value reading—buy books, and give and receive them as gifts.
- Make reading exciting—show that books are full of good ideas kids can use.
- Let kids choose their reading material (at the library, bookstore, etc.),

- Read ghost stories to kids.
- Read detective stories and have kids guess whodunit.
- Get subscriptions in kids' names to magazines focusing on topics they like.
- Have kids read to a family member or friend who can't read anymore.
- Give rewards for reading—a new book or gift certificate from a bookstore, art supplies, tickets to a play or event, a trip to a zoo or museum, an opportunity to stay up late to read.
- Keep a publicly visible list at home showing reading progress (how many books in how much time).
- Have a book scavenger hunt—kids circle objects as they find them in a story.
- Hang up a world map or a U.S. map and have a contest to see who can read more books about or taking place in more different places (cities, countries, etc.).
- Make a time line and have kids read historical novels that fit, marking it as appropriate.
- Obtain a historical map, then get books that describe different points.

Book lovers never go to bed alone.
—ANON

- Make a family card catalog to keep track of what family members have read.
- Have kids help with recipes and actually read them aloud to you as you cook.
- Have kids find and choose recipes of their own and make them together.
- Ask kids to read nutrition labels to you. Make it fun: Say, "Who can tell me which one has more calories?" etc.

- Have kids make their own fortune cookies . . . with fortunes they typed or printed on small pieces of paper.
- Have a contest to see who can write the most disgusting recipe.
- Make a family cookbook.
- Let kids read catalogs to pick out gifts for themselves and others.
- Let kids clip coupons and keep the money that's saved as long as they help with shopping.
- Have kids make shopping lists.
- Have kids make a family telephone and address book.
- Wherever you and kids travel, before and after, have kids read about the place.
- Let kids listen to books on tape in the car. (Good books!)
- Let kids read the map and help navigate.
- On the road: Have kids find words containing every letter of the alphabet—one letter per word.
- Have kids help with a family journal or scrapbook of the family's trips.
- Cut up a newspaper and ask kids to make the funniest mismatch of a story and a headline.
- Play board games that involve reading.

One of the greatest creations of the human mind is the art of reviewing books without having read them.
—G. C. LICHTENBERG

- Create a place in the home that's set up for reading (a special nook with shelves, etc.).
- Make a special children's library section in your home.

- Ask kids their interpretations of current events—leave newspapers around for them to read.
- Ask kids to collect and read movie reviews before the family decides which movie to see.
- Collect books on a theme that will get kids psyched up to read more—like dinosaurs or space travel.
- Suggest that your kids read the book before (or after) seeing the movie about it.
- If kids see something interesting on TV, get a book about the topic.
- Suggest party and Halloween costumes based on book characters.
- Make a family scrapbook and have kids write entries, captions, etc.
- Take a library tour with your kids.
- Sign kids up for library reading hours.
- Go to the zoo or museum, then get books on topics kids liked.
- Get kids excited about history reading by suggesting they search through old newspapers for details about your town in the olden days.
- Have kids make a map of their favorite area around the home, town, a vacation spot, etc.
- Have kids attend bookstore events, like signings, readings, etc.
- Take kids to college or university campuses for events, picnics, sports, etc.—to get them used to the atmosphere of higher learning and the books involved.
- Take turns as a family reading funny books and essays aloud. Entertain one another instead of watching TV.
- Encourage friendships with other kids who like to read.

Some men borrow books; some men steal books; and others beg presentation copies from the author.
—JAMES JEFFREY ROCHE

- Have kids make a book of their favorite limericks or nursery rhymes or jokes.
- Have kids use how-to books to build things, make gifts, do projects, learn a sport, etc.
- Give gifts of a book and the things the book talks about—like a cookbook and ingredients for a recipe, an astronomy book and a star chart, a nature book and a magnifying glass, a book about camping and a compass.
- Do crossword puzzles with kids—or give them as gifts.
- Make a family Trivial Pursuit game based on your family trivia; have kids draw up cards.
- Make a Trivial Pursuit game based on kids' favorite books.
- Have a bring-your-own-book slumber party.
- Have kids write their own sequels to favorite books or stories.
- Get a "why?" book and quiz each other: "Why is the sky blue?"
- Have kids write a family holiday letter or newsletter.
- Have kids write their own letter explaining their absences from school and other things for which letters from home are needed.
- Have kids design their own stationery, get it photocopied, and encourage them to write letters and thank-you notes.
- Encourage kids to develop pen pals.
- Write a letter that everyone adds to and pass it on among family members and friends.

214 / Wendy M. Williams, Ph.D.

- Always have kids write thank-you notes for gifts immediately—before they are allowed to use the gifts!
- Have magazines, young-adult novels, and newspapers around the house.
- Ask kids to recommend books for others to read or to buy as gifts for others.
- Have kids role-play characters from stories, by reading aloud, dressing up and using props, performing the book's dialogue, etc.
- Have kids read to their younger siblings, friends, and relatives.
- Encourage kids to read aloud to you whenever possible to develop their skills and confidence.
- Tell kids about a book you just read that they might like—whet their appetites, read a small section, then leave the book around where they can read it.
- Ask kids often their opinions of books they're reading.
- Use positive peer pressure—get your kids into play groups or social settings with avid readers.
- Encourage kids to read anything in the newspaper at all—even horoscopes, letters to the editor, comics, movie reviews, anything!
- Let kids read short stories instead of longer books—they'll get a greater sense of completion and gratification.
- Encourage kids to write their own plays or other works.
- Encourage kids to read in bed before sleeping every night.

The things I want to know are in books; my best friend is the man who'll get me a book I ain't read.
—ABRAHAM LINCOLN